C000154011

Londoners ....S

A GENEALOGICAL GUIDE

SECOND EDITION

BY

STUART A. RAYMOND

Published by the
Federation of Family History Societies (Publications) Ltd.,
Units 15-16 Chesham Industrial Estate,
Oram Street, Bury, Lancashire, BL9 6EN

Copies also available from:
S.A. & M.J. Raymond, P.O.Box 35, Exeter, EX1 3YZ.

First edition 1994
Second edition 2001

ISBN: 1 86006 129 X FFHS (Publications) Ltd.
ISBN: 1 899668 17 9 S.A. & M.J. Raymond

Printed and Bound by The Alden Group, Oxford and Northampton.

Contents

Front cover illustrations

London Pavement Artist

Introduction

A considerable amount of occupational information on Londoners is available in print. These include biographical dictionaries, record publications, guild histories, archival guides, trade directories, regimental histories, *etc, etc.* All of these help us to identify people in the past, and may provide essential clues in tracing our family trees. The purpose of this bibliography is to draw these publications to the attention of the genealogist. Arrangement is alphabetical by occupation.

London, for the purposes of this work, comprises the area within the historic boundaries of the City of London and the County of Middlesex.

The term 'occupation' is here interpreted broadly to include status as well; titles concerning insurance policy holders, victims, diners, *etc.* are therefore included. With a few exceptions, works listed in my *Occupational sources for genealogists* and *London and Middlesex: a genealogical bibliography* are excluded.

All serious researchers will also consult the extensive:

CREATON, HEATHER. *Bibliography of published works on London history to 1939.* Library Association, 1994.

Many books on occupations in London simply describe or analyse a particular trade, but give no information of genealogical value. Such works are, in general, excluded here.

Much occupational information is given in business house histories. A few of these are listed here; for a comprehensive — although now rather outdated — listing, see:

GUILDHALL LIBRARY. *London business house histories: a handlist.* Corporation of London Library Committee, 1964.

Many works listed here relate to the London livery companies. In their day, these were important institutions for their particular trades. It should be noted, however, that modern livery companies often have only tenuous connection with particular occupations. This is not a comprehensive listing of company histories. For that, reference should be made to:

KAHL, WILLIAM F. *The development of London livery companies: an historical essay and a select bibliography.* Kress Library of Business and Economics publication 15. Boston: Baker Library, Harvard Graduate School of Business Administration, 1960.

This is supplemented by:

KAHL, WILLIAM F. 'A checklist of books, pamphlets and broadsides on the London livery companies', *Gl.M.* **2**(3), 1962, 99-126.

Works on the livery companies frequently provide much more than purely occupational information. Companies frequently owned estates and administered charities, they had contact with tenants, benefactors and pensioners, they paid other tradesmen to cater for their feasts. Many works dealing with these activities are listed here; a few more are listed in *London and Middlesex: a genealogical bibliography.*

The archives of the livery companies survive in bulk; these reflect the companies' diverse activities. The standard guide is:

GUILDHALL LIBRARY. *City livery companies and related organisations: a guide to their archives in Guildhall Library.* 3rd ed. Guildhall Library, 1989.

See also:

COOPER, C.R.H. 'The archives of the City of London livery companies and related organisations', *Archives* **16**(72), 1984, 323-53.

In 1884, a major inquiry into the activities of the livery companies was conducted. The report of this inquiry includes a huge mass of information, giving many names of benefactors, tenants, pensioners, *etc.* See:

CITY OF LONDON LIVERY COMPANIES COMMISSION. *Report and appendix.* 5 vols. House of Commons parliamentary papers, 1884, XXXIX.

There are many general histories of the City livery companies. A small selection only can be listed here:

DITCHFIELD, P.H. *The city companies of London and their good works: a record of their history, charity and treasure.* J.M. Dent & Co., 1904. General.

DITCHFIELD, P.H. *The story of the city companies.* G.T. Foulis & Co., 1926. Includes chapters on each of the 12 major companies.

DOOLITTLE, I.G. *The City of London and its livery companies.* Dorchester: Gavin Press, 1982. A detailed history with a useful bibliography.

HAZLITT, W. CAREW. *The livery companies of the City of London: their origin, character, development, and social and political importance.* Swan Sonnenschein & Co., 1892. General.

HERBERT, WILLIAM. *The history of the twelve great livery companies of London, principally compiled from their grants and records, with an historical essay and accounts of each Company, its origin, contribution, government, dress, customs, halls, and trust estates and charities ...* 2 vols. The author, 1836-7. Frequently inaccurate, but nevertheless important; covers the Mercers, Grocers, Drapers, Fishmongers, Goldsmiths, Skinners, Merchant Taylors, Haberdashers, Salters, Ironmongers, Vintners and Clothworkers. Notes many names, but unfortunately these are not indexed.

LANG, JENNIFER. *Pride without prejudice: the story of London's guilds and livery companies.* Perpetua Press, 1975. Popular history.

MELLING, JOHN KENNEDY. *Discovering London's guilds and liveries.* Aylesbury: Shire, 1973. Brief introduction.

THORNLEY, JOHN CHARLES, & HASTINGS, GEORGE, eds. *The guilds of the city of London and their liverymen, being an historical account of the various guilds of the City of London and their liverymen compiled from authentic records.* London & Counties Press Association, [1911]. Includes many brief biographies.

UNWIN, GEORGE. *The gilds and companies of London.* 4th ed. Frank Cass & Co., 1963. Includes list of printed and manuscript records.

VEALE, ELSPETH. 'The great twelve: mistery and fraternity in thirteenth century London', *Historical research* **64**, 1991, 237-63.

An eighteenth century list of livery company members is printed in:

TOMLINS, THOMAS. *List of the Livery of London, with their places of abodes, and businesses, under the heads of the respective companies ...* The author, [1775].

There are many other contemporary lists of members. In general, these have been excluded from this bibliography, since they are held in very few libraries. Many - especially for the nineteenth and twentieth centuries - may be identified by consulting the British Library's *General catalogue of printed books* under the heading, London II: Civic and Municipal Institutions. Livery Companies.

The great majority of the works listed here are readily available in major reference libraries throughout the English-speaking world - you do not have to visit London to consult them. If the particular item you require is not available in your library, you should ask the librarian to obtain it for you on inter-library loan, or at least to tell you where you can obtain a copy. Any reference library worth its salt should be able to provide the latter information.

In compiling this bibliography, I have visited many libraries. Extensive use has been made of the resources of Devon County Library, Exeter University

Library, the British Library, and Guildhall Library; the Greater London History Library and the Bishopsgate Institute have also provided useful information, and my thanks go to the librarians of these institutions for their assistance. Brian Christmas has bombarded me with suggestions of items worth including in this and other books in the *British genealogical bibliographies* series. The book has been seen through the press by Bob Boyd. All these people deserve my thanks. Any errors that remain — and I am sure there will be some - are my sole responsibility, and I would be grateful if they could be brought to my attention. If you come across any work I have omitted which you think ought to be included, please let me know.

Stuart A. Raymond

Bibliographic Presentation

Authors' names are in SMALL CAPITALS. Book and journal titles are in *italics*. Articles appearing in journals, and material such as parish register transcripts, forming only part of books are in inverted commas and textface type. Volume numbers are in **bold** and the individual number of the journal may be shown in parentheses. These are normally followed by the place of publication (except where this is London, which is omitted), the name of the publisher and the date of publication. In the case of articles, further figures indicate page numbers.

Abbreviations

B.T.L.H.S.	Borough of Twickenham Local History Society
C.A.	*Cockney ancestor*
E.H.H.S.	Edmonton Hundred Historical Society
Gl.M.	*Guildhall miscellany*
G.S.L.H.	*Guildhall Studies in London History*
H.C.M.	*Home counties magazine*
J.S.S.L.H.S.	*Journal of the Shepperton and Sunbury Local History Society*
J.H.H.L.H.S.	*Journal of the Hayes and Harlington Local History Society*
L.R.S.	London Record Society
L.T.R.	*London topographical record*
M.G.H.	*Miscellanea genealogica et heraldica*
M.H.N.Q.	*Middlesex and Hertfordshire notes & queries*
M.L.H.C.B.	*Middlesex Local History Council bulletin*
N.M.	*The North Middlesex: journal of the North Middlesex Family History Society*
N.S.	New Series
P.Hg.S.L.	Publications of the Huguenot Society of London
Pr.Hug.Soc.L.	*Proceedings of the Huguenot Society of London*
R.N.E.	*Ruislip, Northwood & Eastcote Local History Society journal*
T.L.M.A.S.	*Transactions of the London and Middlesex Archaeological Society*
W.M.	*West Middlesex Family History Society journal*

Actors and Actresses

Bibliography

HOWARD, DIANA. *Directory of theatre research resources in Greater London.* British Theatre Institute, 1974. Supplement, 1978.

'Handlist of books in Guildhall Library on the London theatre', *GI.M.* 4(2), 1972, 121-35. Lists many works likely to reveal biographical and genealogical information.

Biographical Dictionaries

HIGHFILL, PHILIP H., BURNIM, KALMAN A., & LANGHANS, EDWARD A. *A biographical dictionary of actors, actresses, musicians, dancers, managers, & other stage personnel in London, 1660-1800.* Many vols. Carbondale: Southern Illinois University Press, 1974-. Biographical notes on 8500 individuals; incomplete.

NUNGEZER, EDWIN. *A dictionary of actors and of other persons associated with the public representation of plays in England before 1642.* New Haven: Yale University Press, 1929. Reprinted New York: Greenwood Press, 1968. Mainly Londoners.

Plays and players

The London stage, 1660-1800: a calendar of plays, entertainments & afterpieces, together with casts, box-receipts and contemporary comment ... 5 pts in 11 vols. Carbondale: Southern Illinois University Press, 1960-68.

BAKER, MICHAEL J.N. *The rise of the Victorian actor.* Croom Helm, 1978. Includes 'tables showing the principal biographical details of three generations of actors and actresses who appeared on the stage in the period 1830-90'; also various pedigrees.

BENTLEY, GERALD EADES. 'Players in the parish of St. Giles in the Fields', *Review of English studies* 6, 1930, 149-66. Includes many extracts from the parish registers, early 17th c.

FYVIE, JOHN. *Comedy queens of the Georgian era.* Constable, 1906. 12 brief biographies.

SHERSON, ERROLL. *London's lost theatres of the nineteenth century, with notes on plays and players seen there.* New York: Benjamin Blom, 1969. Originally published 1925. Includes extensive index of personal names.

MULLIN, DONALD. *Victorian plays: a record of significant productions on the London stage, 1837-1901.* New York: Greenwood, 1987. Lists plays with leading actors.

WEARING, J.P. *The London stage, 1890-1899: a calendar of plays and players.* 2 vols. Metuchen: Scarecrow, 1976. Daily listing of plays and players.

WILSON, JOHN HAROLD. *All the Kings ladies: actresses of the Restoration.* Chicago: Chicago University Press, 1958. Includes biographical dictionary of actresses.

Dramatic records

BOSWELL, ELEANORE, & CHAMBERS, E.K. 'Dramatic records: the Lord Chamberlains Office', *Malone Society collections* 2(3), 1931, 321-416. See also index, 417-38. Gives many names of actors, early 17th c.

CHAMBERS, E.K., & GREG, W.W., eds. 'Dramatic records of the City of London: the Remembrancia', *Malone Society collections* 1, 1907, 43-100. Texts of City official documents relating to the theatre. Also includes list of mayors, 1580-1640.

MILL, ANNA J., & CHAMBERS, E.K. 'Dramatic records of the City of London: the repertories, journals and letter books', *Malone Society collections* 2(3), 1931, 285-320. See also index 417-38.

ROBERTSON, JEAN, & GORDON, D.J., eds. *A calendar of dramatic records in the books of the Livery Companies of the City of London, 1485-1640.* Malone Society collections 3, 1954.

ROBERTSON, JEAN. 'A calendar of dramatic records in the books of the London Clothworkers' Company', *Malone Society collections* 5, 1959 (1960), 1-16.

Particular Companies and Theatres

BROWNSTEIN, OSCAR L. 'The Duke's Company in 1667', *Theatre notebook* 28, 1974, 18-23. Residents of Dorset Garden Theatre in St. Brides.

EDMOND, MARY. 'Pembroke's men', *Review of English studies* 25, 1974, 129-36. Discussion of the will of Simon Jewell, 1592, and the light it throws on a company of players.

GAIR, REAVLEY. *The children of Paul's: the story of a theatre company, 1553-1608.* Cambridge: Cambridge University Press, 1982.

11

KNIGHT, WILLIAM G. *A major London 'Minor': the Surrey Theatre, 1805-1865.* Society of Theatre Research, 1997. Includes much information on personnel, with 'Surrey Theatre pay-list for week ending Friday 18 October, 1861'.

RUTTER, CAROL CHILLINGTON, ed. *Documents of the Rose Playhouse.* Manchester: Manchester University Press, 1984. Includes accounts, with names of persons associated with the theatre.

Aldermen
See Mayors, Sheriffs, Aldermen and Councillors

Antiquaries
BRABROOK, EDWARD WILLIAM. 'On the fellows of the Society of Antiquaries of London who have held the office of director', *Archaeologia* **62**, 1910, 59-80. Brief biographies of 26 directors.

EVANS, JOAN. *A history of the Society of Antiquaries.* Oxford: Charles Batey for the Society of Antiquaries, 1956. Includes list of fellows re-elected in 1751.

Apothecaries
BARRETT, C.R.B. *The history of the Society of Apothecaries of London.* Elliot Stock, 1905. General history; includes list of benefactors 18-20th c.

COPEMAN, W.S.C. *The Worshipful Society of Apothecaries of London: a history, 1617-1967.* Oxford: Pergamon Press, 1967. Includes biographical notes on eminent apothecaries.

CAMERON, H. CHARLES. *A history of the Worshipful Society of Apothecaries of London,* ed. E. Ashworth Underwood. Publications **8**. Oxford University Press for the Wellcome Historical Medical Museum, 1963. v.1617-1815. No more published. Detailed study, with extensive notes on sources, and many names.

MATTHEWS, LESLIE G. 'London's immigrant apothecaries, 1600-1800', *Medical history* **18**, 1974, 262-74.

MATTHEWS, LESLIE G. *The royal apothecaries.* Wellcome Historical Medical Library, 1967.

MATTHEWS, LESLIE G. 'Royal apothecaries of the Tudor period', *Medical history* **8**, 1964, 170-80. General discussion.

WALLIS, PATRICK. *London apprentices, vol.32. Apothecaries Company, 1617-1669.* Society of Genealogists, 2000. Not seen.

WHITTET, THOMAS DOUGLAS. *Clerks, bedels and chemical operators of the Society of Apothecaries: the Gideon De Laune lecture for 1977.* E.R. Squibb & Sons, 1979. Brief biographical notes.

See also Pepperers

Apprentices
GOLLAND, JIM. *The Harrow apprentices (1648-1871): a list of Harrow inhabitants whose apprenticeship fees were paid either by the governors of Harrow School, from 1648 to 1871, or by the parish of Harrow from 1705 to 1803.* London Borough of Harrow, 1981.

KAHL, WILLIAM F. 'Apprenticeship and the freedom of the London livery companies, 1690-1750', *Gl.M.* **1**(7), 1952-60, 17-20. General discussion.

SCHWARZ, LEONARD. 'London apprentices in the seventeenth century: some problems', *Local population studies* **38**, 1987, 18-22. Brief general discussion.

SMITH, STEVEN R. 'The social and geographical origins of the London apprentices, 1630-1660', *Gl.M.* **4**(4), 1973, 195-206. General.

WILD, MICHAEL. 'Finding out about 18th century London apprentices', *W.M.* **7**(1), 1988, 5-6.

WAGNER, MARY. 'Hillingdon parish apprentices', *Hillingdon Family History Society magazine* **36**, 1996, 35-6; **37**, 1997, 30-32. List, 18th c.

WEBB, CLIFF. 'City of London apprenticeships and livery company records', *Genealogists' magazine* **26**(1), 1998, 1-4.

See also under particular trades.

Architects
HANSON, MICHAEL. *Famous architects of the city of London: a series of articles first published in the City Press (with map of City Square Mile).* City Press, 1971.

SERVICE, ALASTAIR. *The architects of London and their buildings from 1066 to the present day.* Architectural Press, 1979. A biographical and architectural study.

See also Local Government Officers and Painters.

Armourers

DILLON, HAROLD. 'Armourers and cutlers in 1537', *Reliquary* 3, 1889, 129-32. Includes list of members of two London companies.

FFOULKES, CHARLES. *Some account of the Worshipful Company of Armourers and Brasiers, together with a catalogue of the arms and armour in the possession of the Company.* The Company, 1926. Includes biographical notes on distinguished armourers.

MORLEY, TIMOTHY. *Some account of the Worshipful Company of Armourers and Brasiers in the City of London ...* Waterlow and Sons, 1878. Many names - but no index.

WEBB, CLIFF. *London livery company apprenticeship registers. Volume 22. Armourers and Brasiers Company, c. 1610-1800.* Society of Genealogists, 1998.

'Apprentices and freemen of the Armourers Guild [London] from 1416 to 1621', *Genealogists' magazine* 9, 1940-46, 179-92 & 217-22. List.

Artists

CUST, LIONEL. 'Foreign artists of the Reformed religion working in London from about 1560 to 1660', *Pr.Hug.Soc.L.* 7, 1901-4, 45-82. Many biographical notes, extracts from registers, *etc.*

EDMOND, MARY. 'Limners and picture makers: new light on the lives of miniaturists and large scale portrait painters working in London in the 16th and 17th centuries', *Walpole Society* 47, 1980, 60-242.

HIGGS, JOY. '1861 census', *Hillingdon Family History Society Magazine* 27, 1994, 18-20. List of artists and art students in Kensington.

WALCOT, CYNTHIA. 'Artists - 1823', *Hampshire family historian* 8(4), 1982, 148-9. List of artists in London, with addresses, from a book entitled *The picture of London,* published in 1823.

The painters of Camden Town, 1905-1920. Christie's, 1988.

Bakers

CORNER, GEORGE RICHARD, et al. 'Bakers Hall and the muniments of the Company', *T.L.M.A.S.* 3, 1870, 54-66.

DARE, EDWIN. 'Journeymen bakers in mid-nineteenth century East London', *East London record* 14, 1991, 29-36. General discussion; some names and addresses.

THRUPP, SYLVIA. *A short history of the Worshipful Company of Bakers of London.* Croydon: Galleon Press, 1933. Includes list of masters, 1481-1932, clerks, 1508-1900, and benefactors, 1577-1933, with list of the records of the Company.

YOUNG, SIDNEY. *The Worshipful Company of Bakers of London: the assize of bread, the court of Holymote, etc. Storer's Remembrancia concerning the company.* Furnival Press, 1912. Brief extracts from 13-17th c. records.

YOUNG, SIDNEY. *The Worshipful Company of Bakers of London: a list of the masters and wardens from 1481 to the present time.* Furnival Press, 1912.

See also Wax Chandlers

Bankers

LISLE-WILLIAMS, MICHAEL. 'Merchant banking dynasties in the English class structure: ownership, solidarity and kinship in the City of London, 1850-1960', *British journal of sociology* 35, 1984, 333-62. Lists many names, and includes table showing marital links.

PRICE, F.G. HILTON. *A handbook of London bankers, with some account of their predecessors, the early goldsmiths, together with lists of bankers, from the earliest one printed in 1677, to that of the London Post-Office directory of 1890 ...* Leadenhall Press, 1890-91.

Bank of England

ACRES, W. MARSTON. *The Bank of England from within, 1694-1900.* 2 vols. Oxford University Press, 1931. Includes list of directors.

ACRES, W. MARSTON. 'Directors of the Bank of England', *Notes and queries* 179, 1940, 38-41, 57-62, 80-83, 96-9, 115-8, 131-4, 147-50, 167-70, 182-4 & 200-03. See also 140, 156, 176, 229, 249, 296-8, 354, 391 & 426. Lists 359 directors, with brief biographical notes.

ACRES, W. MARSTON. 'Huguenot directors of the Bank of England', *Pr.Hug.Soc.L.* 15, 1934-7, 238-48. Brief biographies.

13

GUISEPPI, J.A. 'Families of long service at the Bank of England', *Genealogists' magazine* **10**, 1947-50, 399-406 & 439-47.

Coutts & Co
HEALEY, EDNA. *Coutts & Co, 1692-1992: the portrait of a private bank.* Hodder & Stoughton, 1992. Includes pedigree of the descendants of John Campbell, Thomas Coutts, and the Marjoribanks family, with list of directors.

Hoare's Bank
Hoare's Bank: a record, 1673-1932. Privately published, 1932. Includes notes on the Hoare family, with pedigree, and list of customers, 1673-1718.
See also Goldsmiths

Bankrupts
DUFFY, IAN P.H. *Bankruptcy and insolvency in London during the Industrial Revolution.* New York: Garland, 1985. Includes list of bankrupts, 1810-11.

Barbers
DOBSON, JESSIE, & WALKER, R. MILNES. *Barbers and Barber-Surgeons of London: a history of the Barbers and Barber-Surgeons Company of London.* Oxford: Blackwell Scientific, 1979. Includes lists of officers, *etc.*
LAMBERT, GEORGE. 'Barber surgeons', *T.L.M.A.S.* **6**, 1890, 125-89. General history of the Company; includes notes on charities.
THOMAS, JAMES H. 'Hampshire and the Company of Barber-Surgeons, 1658-1720', *Hampshire family historian* **10**(1), 1983, 15-18. Lists apprentices and masters, giving father's names, residences and occupations.
YOUNG, SIDNEY. *The annals of the Barber Surgeons of London.* Blades, East & Blades, 1890. Includes list of masters and wardens, biographical notes on eminent members, including pedigrees of Aylef, Pen, Proby, Lithieullier, *etc.,* and much else.

Barge Masters & Owners
COMPTON, HUGH J. 'Thames barge registers', *Railway and Canal Historical Society journal* **28**, 1986, 353-5. Note on a potentially useful source for barge owners.

SAYLE, R.T.D. *The barges of the Merchant Taylor's Company, with notes on their barge masters, barge houses, and water processions.* Eastern Press, 1933. Includes list of barge masters, 17-19th c.
WOOD, E. 'Brentford barge owners', *Brentford & Chiswick Local History Society journal* **2**, 1981, 17-18. 18-19th c., text of a lecture.

Basket Makers
BOBART, HENRY HODGKINSON. *Records of the Basket Makers Company.* Dunn Collin & Co., 1911. Includes lists of officers, and extracts from original sources.
RONALD, PAUL. *The Basketmakers Company: A History of the Worshipful Company of Basketmakers of the City of London.* The Company, 1978. Includes list of wardens, *etc.* Based on Bobart.
WEBB, CLIFF. *London Livery company apprenticeship registers volume 10. Basketmakers Company 1639-1824.* Society of Genealogists, 1997.

Bell Founders
STAHLSCHMIDT, J.C.L. *Surrey bells and London bell-founders: a contribution to the comparative study of bell inscriptions.* Elliot Stock, 1884.
TYSSEN, AMHERST D. 'The history of the Whitechapel bell-foundry', *T.L.M.A.S.* N.S. **5**, 1929, 195-226. Includes list of bellfounders, 1567-1865.
WALTERS, H.B. 'London church bells and bell-founders', *Transactions of the St. Pauls Ecclesiological Society* **6**, 1906-10, 101-28. Includes names of founders.

Bell Ringers
COOK, W.T. *The Society of College Youths, 1637-1987: a new history of the Society.* Ancient Society of College Youths, 1987. Bell ringers; includes list of masters.
TROLLOPE, J. ARMIGER. *The College Youths: a history of the Society.* Woking: Ringing World, 1937. Bellringers; includes list of masters.

Biologists
GAGE, ANDREW THOMAS, & STEARN, WILLIAM THOMAS. *A bicentenary history of the Linnean Society of London.* The Society, 1988. Includes list of officers.

14

Blacksmiths

ADAMS, ARTHUR. *The history of the Worshipful Company of Blacksmiths, from early times until the year 1785, being selected reproductions from the original books of the Company, an historical introduction, and many notes.* 2nd ed. Sylvan Press, 1951. *See also* Ironmongers

Book Trades

In past times, the roles of printer, publisher, book-binder, stationer, bookseller, *etc.,* were often performed by the same individual. Consequently, works relating to them are listed here together.

General Works

CHRISTIANSON, C. PAUL. 'A community of book artisans in Chaucer's London', *Viator* **20**, 1989, 207-18.

CHRISTIANSON, C. PAUL. 'Early London bookbinders and parchmeners', *Book collector* **34**, 1985, 41-54. General discussion, 14-15th c.

CHRISTIANSON, C. PAUL. 'Evidence for the study of London's late medieval manuscript-book trade', in GRIFFITHS, JEREMY, & PEARSALL, DEREK, eds. *Book-production and publishing in Britain, 1375-1475.* Cambridge: C.U.P., 1989, 87-108. General discussion of the evidence, which may be of genealogical value.

CHRISTIANSON, C. PAUL. *Memorials of the book trade in medieval London: the archives of Old London Bridge.* Manuscript studies 3. D.S. Brewer, 1987. Based on the archives of Bridge House Estates.

DUFF, E. GORDON. *The printers, stationers and bookbinders of Westminster and London from 1476 to 1535.* Cambridge: C.U.P., 1906. General history; many names.

GREEN, LINDA. 'Some notes on researching ancestors in the printing and paper-making trades', *Greentrees: the journal of the Central Middlesex Family History Society* **15**(2), 1996, 36-7.

HOWE, ELLIC, & CHILD, JOHN. *The Society of London bookbinders, 1780-1951.* Sylvan Press, 1952. General history.

HOWE, ELLIC. 'The archives of the London journeymen bookbinders', *The Library* 4th series **25**, 1944-5, 185-6. Brief note.

NIXON, HOWARD M. 'Some Huguenot bookbinders', *Huguenot Society of London proceedings* **23**, 1981, 319-29. 16th c.

PLOMER, H.R. 'Notices of English stationers in the archives of the city of London', *Transactions of the Bibliographical Society* **6**, 1900-1901, 13-27.

TODD, WILLIAM B. 'London printers' imprints, 1800-40', *The Library* 5th series **21**, 1966, 46-62. Includes names of some master printers.

TREADWELL, MICHAEL. 'London printers and printing houses in 1705', *Publishing history* **7**, 1980, 5-44. Biographical notes.

TREADWELL, MICHEAL. 'London trade publishers, 1675-1750', *Library* 6th series **4**, 1982, 99-134. General discussion.

Fleet Street

AVIS, F.C. *Printers of Fleet Street and St.Paul's Churchyard in the sixteenth century.* Glenview Press, 1964. Includes lists.

New Bond Street

SMITH, GEORGE, & BENGER, FRANK. *The oldest London bookshop: a history of two hundred years.* Ellis, 1928. Traces the descent of 29, New Bond Street.

St. Giles, Cripplegate

MILLER, WILLIAM E. 'Printers and stationers in the parish of St. Giles, Cripplegate, 1561-1640', *Studies in bibliography* **19**, 1966, 15-38. List.

St.Paul's Churchyard

BLAYNEY, PETER W.H. *The bookshops in Paul's Cross churchyard.* Occasional papers of the Bibliographical Society 5, 1990. Gives many names of booksellers, *etc.*

WELCH, CHARLES. 'St.Paul's Cathedral and its early literary associations', *T.L.M.A.S.* N.S. **1**, 1905, 74-114. Includes list of printers with biographical notes.

WHEATLEY, H.B. 'Signs of booksellers in St.Paul's Churchyard', *Transactions of the Bibliographical Society* **9**, 1906-8, 67-106. Includes list of names, arranged by sign.

Biographical Dictionaries, Directories and Lists

BROWN, PHILIP A.H. *London publishers and printers c.1800-1870.* British Library, 1982. List.

CHRISTIANSON, C. PAUL. *Directory of London stationers and book artisans, 1300-1500*. New York: Bibliographical Society of America, 1990. Detailed biographical dictionary.

HEAL, AMBROSE. 'London booksellers and publishers, 1700-50: supplementary notes', *Notes and queries* **161**, 1931, 93-9, 169-73, 240-44, 313-6, 328-9, 347-51, 363-7, 382-5, 400-404 & 435-9; **162**, 1932, 116-20. *See also* **162**, 1932, 46-7. Supplements Wood's work listed below.

HOWE, ELLIC. *A list of London bookbinders, 1648-1815*. Bibliographical Society, 1950. Includes biographical notes.

HOWE, ELLIC. *London bookbinders, 1780-1806*. Merrion Press & Desmond Zwemmer, 1988.

HOWE, ELLIC. *The London compositor: documents relating to wages, working conditions and customs of the London printing trade, 1785-1900*. Bibliographical Society, 1947. Includes lists of 1724, 1785 and 1839.

MAXTED, IAN. *The London book trades, 1735-1775: a checklist of members in trade directories and Musgrave's Obituary*. Exeter working papers in book trade history 3. Exeter: J. Maxted, 1984.

MAXTED, IAN. *The London book trades, 1775-1800: a preliminary checklist of members*. Folkestone: Dawson, 1977. For a topographical index to this volume, see: MAXTED, IAN. *The London book trades, 1775-1800: a topographical guide*. Exeter working papers in British book trade history 1. Exeter: J. Maxted, 1980.

MCKENZIE, D.F. 'A list of printers' apprentices 1605-40', *Studies in bibliography* **13**, 1958, 109-41.

PACKER, MAURICE. *Bookbinders of Victorian London*. British Library, 1991. List with brief notes.

PENDRED, JOHN. *The earliest directory of the book trade*. ed. Graham Pollard. Supplement to the Bibliographical Society's transactions **14**, 1955. Originally published 1785. The greater portion of names mentioned are in London.

RAMSDEN, CHARLES. *London bookbinders, 1780-1840*. B.T.Batsford, 1956. List.

TODD, WILLIAM B. *A directory of printers and others in allied trades: London and vicinity, 1800-1840*. Printing Historical Society, 1972. Biographical dictionary.

TREADWELL, MICHAEL. 'Lists of master printers: the size of the London printing trade, 1673-1723' in MYERS, ROBIN, & HARRIS, MICHAEL, eds. *Aspects of printing from 1600*. Oxford: Oxford Polytechnic Press, 1987, 141-70. Includes various lists of names.

TWYMAN, MICHAEL. *A directory of London lithographic printers, 1800-1850*. Printing History Society, 1976. Reprinted from *Journal of the Printing Historical Society* **10**, 1974-5, 1-55. List, giving addresses and notes on sources.

WELCH, CHARLES. 'The city printers', *Transactions of the Bibliographical Society* **14**, 1919, 175-241. List of 19 official printers, with details of works printed, 1517-1864.

WOOD, FREDERICK T. 'Notes on London booksellers and publishers, 1700-1750', *Notes and queries* **161-2**, 1931-2 & **162**, 1932, *passim*. Biographical dictionary. Supplemented by Heal's work listed above. 'Stationers made free of the City in 1551/2 and 1552', *Transactions of the Cambridge Bibliographical Society* **1**, 1949-53, 194-5. Brief list.

Stationers Company

There are several useful general histories of the Company:

BLAGDEN, CYPRIAN. *The Stationers Company: a history, 1403-1959*. Allen & Unwin, 1960. Includes rental of 1773, with names of tenants.

BLAGDEN, CYPRIAN. 'The Stationer's Company in the eighteenth century', *Gl.M.* **1**(10), 1952-9, 36-52. Includes list of the Company's court, 1792, giving ages.

HODGSON, SIDNEY. *The Worshipful Company of Stationers and Newspaper Makers: notes on its origin and history*. The Company, 1953. Includes biographical notes on prominent members, 17-18th c.

POLLARD, GRAHAM. 'The Company of Stationers before 1557', *The Library* 4th series **18**, 1937-8, 1-38. Includes appendix listing known wardens.

RIVINGTON, C.R. *A short account of the Worshipful Company of Stationers ...* [The Company], 1903. Many names; prepared for 500th anniversary celebration.
See also:
TURNER, MICHAEL. 'The personnel of the Stationers Company, 1800-30: work in progress', in MYERS, ROBIN, & HARRIS, MICHAEL, eds. *Economics of the British book trade, 1605-1939.* Cambridge: Chadwyck-Healey, 1985, 78-102.
For the Company's archives, see:
MYERS, ROBIN. *The Stationers' Company archive: an account of the records, 1554-1984.* Winchester: St.Pauls Bibliographies, 1990.
MYERS. R. 'Book trade archives: the records of the Worshipful Company of Stationers and Newspaper Makers (1554-1912)', *Publishing history* **13**, 1983, 89-104.
MYERS. ROBIN. 'The records of the Worshipful Company of Stationers and Newspaper Makers, (1554-1912)', *Archives* **16**(69), 1983, 28-38. General discussion, with list.
RIVINGTON. CHARLES ROBERT. 'The records of the Worshipful Company of Stationers', *T.L.M.A.S.* **6**, 1890, 280-340. Includes list of masters.
'Catalogue of records at Stationers Hall', *The Library* 4th series **6**, 1926, 349-57.
Various records of the Company have been published. Its registers are of particular importance:
ARBER, EDWARD. ed. *A transcript of the registers of the Company of Stationers of London, 1554-1640 A.D.* 5 vols. Gloucester, Massachusetts: Peter Smith, 1967. Originally published 1875-95. Gives names of many printers, booksellers, *etc.* Continued by:
EYRE, G.E. BRISCOE, ed. *A transcript of the registers of the Worshipful Company of Stationers, 1640-1708 A.D.* 3 vols. Roxburghe Club **163**. 1913-14. Reprinted Gloucester, Massachusetts: Peter Smith, 1967.
See also:
GREG, WALTER WILSON, SIR, ed. *A companion to Arber, being a calendar of documents in Edward Arber's transcript of the register of the Company of Stationers of London, 1554-1640.* Oxford: Clarendon Press, 1967.

GREG, WALTER W., SIR. *Licensers for the press &c to 1640: a biographical index based mainly on Arber's 'Transcript of the Registers of the Company of Stationers'.* Oxford Bibliographical Society publications N.S. **10**, 1962.
GREG, W.W. 'Some notes on the Stationers registers', *Bibliographical Society transactions* **7**, 1926-7, 376-86.
Other record publications include:
GREG, W.W., & BOSWELL, E., eds. *Records of the Court of the Stationers Co., 1576 to 1602, from register B.* Bibliographical Society, 1930. Includes lists of masters, wardens and assistants. Continued by:
JACKSON, WILLIAM A., ed. *Records of the Court of the Stationers Company, 1602 to 1640.* Bibliographical Society, 1957.
FERGUSON, W. CRAIG. *The Loan Book of the Stationers Company: with a list of transactions, 1592-1629.* Occasional papers **4**. Bibliographical Society, 1989. Records loans to young men establishing their businesses.
FERGUSON, W. CRAIG. 'The Stationers Company poor book, 1608-1700', *The Library* 5th series, 1975, 37-51. Alphabetical list of members receiving support from the Company's poor fund.
HODSON, S. 'Papers and documents recently found at Stationers Hall', *The Library* 4th series **25**, 1945, 23-36. Description of accounts, court minutes, vouchers, *etc.,* of the Stationers Company, 17th c.
A number of works identify the Company's apprentices:
McKENZIE, D.F. *Stationers Company apprentices, 1605-1640.* Charlottesville: Bibliographical Society of the University of Virginia, 1961.
McKENZIE, D.F. *Stationers Company apprentices, 1641-1700.* Oxford Bibliographical Society publications N.S. **17**, 1974.
McKENZIE, D.F. *Stationers' Company apprentices, 1701-1800.* Oxford Bibliographical Society publications N.S. **19**, 1978.
MORGAN, PAUL. *Warwickshire apprentices in the Stationers Company of London, 1563-1700.* Dugdale Society occasional papers **25**, 1978. Includes 205 brief biographies.
See also Map Sellers.

Bottle Manufacturers
PROCKTER, ADRIAN, & SANDOW, MIKE. *The London mineral water bottle directory, 1870-1914.* London Reference Books, 1985. Alphabetical list.

Bow Street Runners
BABINGTON, ANTHONY. *A house in Bow Street: crime and the magistracy: London, 1740-1881.* Macdonald, 1969. General study.

Bowyers
WEBB, CLIFF. *London livery companies apprenticeship registers, volume 3. Bowyers Company, 1680-1806; Fletchers Company 1739-54; Longbowstringmakers' Company 1604-68, 1709, 1714-17.* Society of Genealogists, 1996.

Brasiers
See Armourers

Brewers
BALL, MIA. *The Worshipful Company of Brewers: a short history.* Hutchinson Benham, 1977. Includes lists of clerks and masters.

HARLEY, J.A.G. 'Samuel Whitbread's first enterprise: a survey of the organisation and methods of an eighteenth century London brewery, 1742-50', *Gl.M.* 1(9), 1952-9, 3-26. Includes list of employees.

WEBB, CLIFF. *London livery company apprenticeship register. Volume 1. Brewers Company, 1685-1800.* Society of Genealogists, 1996.

Bricklayers
See Tylers

Brickmakers
'Brickmakers of West Drayton and Harlington', *Hillingdon Family History Society magazine* 37, 1997, 14-15. List from the 1881 census.

'Hayes brick-workers of 1881', *Hillingdon Family History Society maggazine* 35, 1996, 10-12. List from the census.

Broderers
HOLFORD, CHRISTOPHER. *A chat about the Broderers Company.* George Allen & Sons, 1910. Includes list of freemen from 1694.

LEVY, PERCY R. *Plain dealing fellows: a second chat about the Broderers Company.* Worshipful Company of Broderers, 1986. Includes lists of officers from 1679.

WEBB, CLIFF. *London livery companies apprenticeship registers. Volume 6. Broderers Company. 1679-1713, 1763-1800; Combmakers' Company 1744-50; Fanmakers' Company 1775-1805; Frameworkknitters' Company 1727-30; Fruiterers' Company 1750-1815; Gardeners' Company 1764-1850; Horners' Company 1731-1800.* Society of Genealogists, 1997.

Brokers
ABRAHAMS, DUDLEY. 'Jew brokers of the City of London', in JEWISH HISTORICAL SOCIETY OF ENGLAND *Miscellanies* 3, 1937, 80-94. Includes list, 1657-1800.

ALDOUS, VIVIAN. *Sworn brokers' archives.* Research guide 2. Corporation of Londong Records Office, 1995. 'Brokers' operated as agents or middlemen between merchants.

A list of the brokers of the City of London. Henry Fenwick, 1797. Continued irregularly by various printers until 1886 at least.

Building Tradesmen
BELCHER, VICTOR. 'The records of a London building firm', *Business archives: the journal of the Business Archives Council* N.S., 4, 1982, 25-30. Discussion of the papers of C.A.Daw and Son of Kensington, late 19th c.

WEAVER, L. 'The complete building accounts of the city chambers (parochial) designed by Sir Christopher Wren', *Archaeologia* 66, 1914-15, 1-60. 17th c., includes lists of tradesmen.

'Table of the fifty-four churches, with trades and costs, from the official building accounts', *Wren Society* 10, 1933, 45-55. Lists building tradesmen employed in building the Wren churches after the Great Fire.

Butchers
JONES, PHILIP E. *The butchers of London: a history of the Worshipful Company of Butchers of the City of London.* Secker & Warburg, 1976. Includes lists of wardens, 1544-1605, masters, 1605-1975, clerks, 1544-1975, and apprentices, 1585-9; also of principal records of the Company.

PEARCE, ARTHUR. *The history of the Butchers' Company.* Meat Trades Journal Co., 1929. Includes lists of various officers, 16-20th c.

Carmen
BENNETT, ERIC. *The Worshipful Company of Carmen of London.* New ed. Buckingham: Barracuda, 1982. Includes lists of masters and clerks from 1668.

Carpenters
ALFORD, B.W.E., & BARKER, T.C. *A history of the Carpenters Company.* George Allen and Unwin, 1968. Includes lists of masters, wardens, clerks, and beadles; also many references to original sources.

JUPP, EDWARD BASIL. *An historical account of the Worshipful Company of Carpenters of the City of London, compiled chiefly from records in their possession.* 2nd ed. Pickering & Chatto, 1887. Includes list of masters and wardens, 1438-1885, *etc.*

MARSH, BOWER, et al, eds. *Records of the Worshipful Company of Carpenters.* 7 vols. Oxford: O.U.P., for the Company, 1913-68. Contents: v.1. Apprentices entry book, 1654-1694, ed. Bower Marsh. v.2. Wardens account book, 1438-1516, ed. Bower Marsh. v.3. Court book, 1533-1573, ed. Bower Marsh. v.4. Wardens account book, 1546-1571, ed. Bower Marsh. v.5. Wardens account book, 1571-1591, transcribed by Bower Marsh, ed. John Ainsworth. v.6. Court book, 1573-1594, transcribed by Bower Marsh, ed. John Ainsworth. v.7. Wardens account book, 1592-1614, ed. A.M. Millard.

MARSH, BOWER. 'Apprentices from Dorset bound at Carpenters Hall, London, 1654-1694', *Notes and queries for Somerset and Dorset* 14, 1915, 83-5.

MARSH, BOWER. 'Apprentices from the County of Gloucester bound at Carpenters Hall, London', *Gloucestershire notes and queries* 10, 1914, 76-80. Not continued.

RIDLEY, JASPER. *A history of the Carpenters Company.* Worshipful Company of Carpenters, 1996. Includes lists of masters and warders, and of clerks and beadles, 15-20th c.

'Suffolk apprentices on the books of the Carpenters Company, London, 1655-93', *East Anglian miscellany,* 1917, 64-5 & 66-7.

Carriers
BATES, ALAN. *Directory of stage coach services, 1836.* Newton Abbot: David & Charles, 1969. Timetables, giving many names of carriers.

GERHOLD, DORIAN. 'The growth of the London carrying trade, 1681-1838', *Economic history review* 41, 1988, 392-410. General discussion.

PRIOR, E.H. 'Carter Paterson: roll of honour, 1914-1919', *C.A.* 53, 1991-2, 23-5. Carter Paterson were a firm of carriers.

Cheesemongers
STERN, WALTER M. 'Where oh where are the cheesemongers of London?', *London journal* 5(2), 1979, 228-48. Discussion of the evidence for cheesemongers.

Choristers
GARRETT, KATHLEEN ISABELLA. 'A list of some of St.Paul's Cathedral choristers before 1873' *Guidhall studies in London history* 1(2), 1974, 82-93. Includes brief biographical notes.

LENNAM, TREVOR. 'The children of Paul's, 1551-1582', *Elizabethan theatre* 2, 1970, 20-36. Gives names of choristers of St.Pauls, mid-16th c.

TEMPLARS UNION. *In memoriam.* Temple Church, 1923. World War I roll of honour of the Temple choir, with biographical notes.

Clergy
Two major attempts to list the clergy of the Diocese of London have been made:
NEWCOURT, RIC. *Repertorium ecclesiasticum parochiale Londinense: an ecclesiastical parochial history of the Diocese of London.* 2 vols. Chris Bateman, et al, 1708-10. Vol.1. London and Middlesex, with parts of Hertfordshire. Vol.2. Essex.

HENNESY, GEORGE. *Novum repertorium ecclesiasticum parochiale Londinense, or, London Diocesan clergy succession from the earliest times to the year 1898.* Swan Sonnerscheim, 1898.

For Diocesan dignitaries, consult:
LE NEVE, JOHN. *Fasti ecclesiae Anglicanae, 1066-1300, 1. St.Paul's, London,* comp. Diana E. Greenway. Athlone Press, 1968.
LE NEVE, JOHN. *Fasti ecclesiae Anglicanae, 1300-1541, 5. St.Paul's, London,* comp. Joyce M. Horn. Athlone Press, 1969.
LE NEVE, JOHN. *Fasti ecclesiae Anglicanae, 1541-1857, 1: St.Paul's, London,* comp. Joyce M. Horn. Athlone Press, 1969.
Much further information on clergy — both Anglican and nonconformist — is available in print. Of particular importance are the published diocesan records, and the numerous lists of clergy of particular parishes. These are all listed in my *London and Middlesex: a genealogical bibliography,* especially in section 10 (2nd edition).

Clockmakers
ATKINS, CHARLES EDWARD. *Register of apprenticeships of the Worshipful Company of Clockmakers of the City of London, from its incorporation in 1631 to its tercentenary in 1931 ...* Privately printed, 1931.
ATKINS, SAMUEL ELLIOTT, & OVERALL, WILLIAM HENRY. *Some account of the Worshipful Company of Clockmakers of the City of London.* Blades, East & Blades, 1881. Extensive history, noting many names, and including list of masters and wardens, 1632-1880, but without an index.
BROMLEY, JOHN. *The Clockmakers library: the catalogue of the books and manuscripts in the library of the Worshipful Company of Clockmakers.* Sotheby Parke Bernet, 1977. Includes listing of the Company's archives, which include much material on clockmakers.
MORGAN, C. OCTAVIUS. 'List of members of the Clockmakers' Company of London, from the period of their incorporation in 1631 to the year 1732', *Archaeological journal* **40**, 1883, 193-214.
Freemen of the Worshipful Company of Clockmakers, 1631-1984. Riversdale, Isle of Man: G.Daniels, 1984. List.

Cloth Workers
GIRTIN, THOMAS. *The golden ram: a narrative history of the Clothworkers Company, 1528-1958.* The Company, 1956. Includes biographical notes on 'some Clothworker personalities', with list of masters from 1536.
The ordinances of the Cloth Workers' Company, together with those of the ancient guilds or fraternities of the Fullers & Shearmen of the City of London. Wyman & Sons, 1881. Includes some names.
SCHMIECHEN, J.A. *Sweated industries and sweated labour: the London clothing trades, 1860-1914.* Croom Helm, 1984. General history, citing many useful references.
WEINSTEIN, ROSEMARY. 'Clothworkers in St.Stephen Coleman parish, 1612', *London topographical record* **24**, 1980, 61-80. Discussion of a survey of the Clothworkers Company estate.

Club Members
ALLEN, ROBERT JOSEPH. *The clubs of Augustus London.* Hamden, Connecticut: Anchor Books, 1967. Originally published, 1933. General history.
TIMBS, JOHN. *Clubs and club-life in London, with anecdotes of its famous coffee-houses, hostelries and taverns.* Chatto and Windus, 1872. Anecdotal study of numerous clubs; little of direct genealogical interest.

Athenaeum
WAUGH, FRANCIS GLEDSTANES. *Members of the Athenaeum Club from its foundation.* Privately printed, [1899?]

Garrick Club
BARHAM, R.H. *The Garrick Club: notices of one hundred and thirty-five of its former members ...* New York: Privately printed, 1896.

Saville Club
SEAMAN, O., SIR. *The Saville Club, 1868 to 1923.* The Club, 1923. Includes 'Chronological list of members 1868 to 1923'.

Society of Dilettante

CUST, LIONEL. *History of the Society of Dilettanti,* ed. Sidney Colvin. Macmillan and Co., 1898. Includes list of members, 1736-1897, with brief biographical notes.

FRASER, WILLIAM, SIR. ed. *Members of the Society of Dilettanti, 1736-1874.* Chiswick Press, 1874.

HARCOURT-SMITH, CECIL, SIR. *The Society of Dilettanti: its regalia and pictures.* Macmillan and Co., for the Society, 1932. Includes MACMILLAN, GEORGE A. 'An outline of its history 1914-1932, and a list of members elected during that period'.

Union Club

ROME,R.C. *Union Club: an illustrated descriptive record of the oldest members club in London, founded circa 1799.* B.T.Batsford, 1948. Includes various lists of members.

White's

COLSON, PERCY. *White's, 1693-1950* William Heinemann, 1951. Includes 'a complete list of members from 1736 to 1950'.

Coachmakers

NOCKOLDS, HAROLD, ed. *The coachmakers: a history of the Worshipful Company of Coachmakers and Coach Harness Makers, 1677-1977.* J.A. Allen, 1977. Includes list of masters and clerks.

WEBB, CLIFF. ed. *London livery company apprenticeship registers. Volume 23. Coachmakers and Coach Harness Makers Company, 1677-1800.* Society of Genealogists, 1998.

A history of the Worshipful Company of Coachmakers and Coach Harness-Makers of London. Chapel River Press, 1937. Includes list of masters and clerks, 1677-1936, *etc.*

Coal Factors

SMITH, RAYMOND. *Sea-coal for London: history of the coal factors in the London market.* Longmans, 1961. Includes list of members of the Coal Factors Society, 1772-1955.

Coffee House Proprietors

LILLYWHITE, BRYANT. *London coffee houses: a reference book of coffee houses of the seventeenth, eighteenth and nineteenth centuries.* George Allen and Unwin, 1963. Gazetteer of 2034 coffee houses, giving names of many proprietors.

See also Tradesmen.

Combmakers

BOWERS, RON. *Combs, combmakers, and the Combmakers Company.* Honiton: the author, 1987. Includes list of combmakers in London, with dates and some addresses.

See also Broderers

Compositors

See Book Trades

Convicts

DIXON, WILLIAM HEPWORTH. *The London prisons, with an account of the more distinguished persons who have been confined in them.* Jackson and Walford, 1850. Reprinted Garland, 1985.

LINEBAUGH, PETER. *The London hanged: crime and civil society in the eighteenth century.* Allen Lane, 1991. A general history, with useful references.

There are many editions of the *Newgate Calendar,* which reports numerous notorious trials. Some of the more easily available works include:

BIRKETT, NORMAN, SIR. ed. *The Newgate calendar.* Folio Society, 1951.

HEPPENSTALL, RAYNER. *Reflections on the Newgate calendar.* W.H.Allen, 1975. Includes a useful bibliography.

KNAPP, ANDREW, & BALDWIN, WILLIAM. *The Newgate Calendar, comprising interesting memoirs of the most notorious characters who have been convicted of outrages on the laws of England since the commencement of the eighteenth century ...* 4 vols. J. Robins & Co., 1824-6.

LAURIE, B., [ed.] *The Newgate calendar, or, malefactors' bloody register ...* T. Werner Laurie, 1932.

MITCHELL, EDWIN VALENTINE, ed. *The Newgate Calendar, containing interesting memoirs of the most notorious characters who have been convicted of outrages on the laws of England ...* John Lane, 1928.
RAYNER, L., & CROOK, G.T., eds. *The complete Newgate calendar.* 5 vols. Navarre Society, 1926.
WILKINSON, GEORGE THEODORE. *The Newgate calendar improved, being interesting memoirs of notorious characters who have been convicted of offences against the laws of England during the seventeenth century ...* R. Evans, 1816. Reprinted, with an introduction by Christopher Hibbert, as *The Newgate Calendar.* Cardinal, 1991.
See also:
BABINGTON, ANTHONY. *The English Bastille: a history of Newgate gaol, and prison conditions in Britain, 1188-1902.* Macdonald, 1971. General study; with bibliography.
See also Debtors

Cooks
HERBAGE, PETER FREDERICK. *The Cooks and the City of London: a history of the Worshipful Company of Cooks, London.* The Company, 1982. Includes lists of officers; also lists of members in 1538 and 1982.
PHILLIPS, F. TAVERNER. *A history of the Worshipful Company of Cooks, London.* [ ], 1932. Many names, 14-20th c.
PHILLIPS, FRANK TAVERNER. *A second history of the Worshipful Company of Cooks, London.* The Company, 1966. Includes many names.
WEBB, CLIFF. *London livery company apprenticeship registers volume 26. Cook's Company, 1654-1800.* Society of Genealogists, 1999.

Coopers
ELKINGTON, GEORGE. *The Coopers: company and craft.* Sampson, Low, Marston & Co., [1933]. General history.
FIRTH, JAMES F., ed. *Coopers Company: historical memoranda, charters, documents, and extracts from the records of the Corporation and the books of the Company, 1396-1848.* Arthur Taylor, 1848.

FOSTER, SIR WILLIAM. *A short history of the Worshipful Company of Coopers of London.* Cambridge: C.U.P., 1944. Includes biographical notes on prominent members.
JACKSON, JOHN. *Notes on the history and antiquities of the Worshipful Company of Coopers.* Eden Fisher & Co., 1914. Brief account, but includes list of brethren, 1440.

Cordwainers
LANG, JENNIFER. *The Worshipful Company of Cordwainers, 1439-1979.* Perpetua Press, 1980. Includes list of masters and clerks.
MANDER, C.H. WATERLAND. *A descriptive and historical account of the Guild of Cordwainers of the City of London.* The Company, 1931. Includes list of masters and wardens.

Coroners
See Medical Professions

Cotton Spinners
GIBBENS, LILIAN. 'Child pauper apprentices sent to Messrs William Toplis & Company, cotton spinners of Nottinghamshire', *N.M.* **13**, 1991, 111-14. Includes list of apprentices from Tottenham, Islington and Holborn, 1786-1805.

Councillors
See Mayors, Sheriffs, Aldermen and Councillors

Cricketers
ASHLEY-COOPER,F.S. *Middlesex County Cricket Club, vol. II: 1900-20.* William Heinemann, 1921. Many names.
ASSOCIATION OF CRICKET STATISTICIANS. *Middlesex cricketers, 1850-1976.* Hampton in Arden: The Association, 1976. Includes list of cricketers with brief biographical notes.
FORD, W.J. *Middlesex County Cricket Club, 1864-1899.* Longmans Green & Co., 1900. Includes list of players, giving dates of births and deaths.
HEALD, BRIAN. *Middlesex County Cricket Club first-class records, 1850-1998.* Sleaford: Limlow Books, 1999. Includes numerous lists of names.
HEAVENS, ROGER. *An index to M.C.C. cricket scores and biographies.* Little Eversden: the author, 1996. Not seen.

LEMMON, DAVID. *The official history of Middlesex County Cricket Club.* Christopher Helm, 1988. Includes 'biographical details of Middlesex cricketers, giving dates of birth and death, and place of birth'.

Curriers

BURKITT, E.H. *A short history of the Worshipful Company of Curriers.* Rev.ed. The Company, 1923. Includes list of masters, 1682-1906.

MAYER, EDWARD. *The Curriers and the City of London: a history of the Worshipful Company of Curriers.* Curwen Press for the Company, 1968. Includes list of masters, *etc.*

Cutlers

GIRTIN, TOM. *The mark of the sword: a narrative history of the Cutlers' Company, 1189-1925.* Hutchinson Benham, 1975. Includes list of masters.

WELCH, CHARLES. *History of the Cutlers Company of London, and of the minor cutlery crafts, with biographical notices of early London cutlers.* 2 vols. The Company, 1916-23.
See also Armourers

Dairymen

EASTON, E.G. *The metropolitan dairymen's directory and hand-book of reference for 1886 ... including separate lists of dairymen, cowkeepers, purveyors of milk, comprising the whole of the dairymen in the metropolis ...* Cowkeeper & Dairyman's Journal, 1886.

Dancers
See Actors

Debaters
Laws and transactions of the London Debating Society, with a list of the members connected up to November 1st, 1826. Richard Taylor, 1826.

Debtors

INNES, JOANNA. 'The King's Bench prison in the later eighteenth century: law, authority and order in a London debtors prison', in BREWER, JOHN, & STYLES, JOHN, eds. *An ungovernable people: the English and their law in the seventeenth and eighteenth centuries.* Hutchinson, 1980, 250-98.

Dentists
See Medical Professions

Diners
The Lowtonian Society, founded in the year 1793. [The Society], 1908. Includes list of members of a dining club.

Distillers

WEBB, CLIFF. *London livery company apprenticeship registers. Volume II. Distillers' Company, 1659-1811.* Society of Genealogists, 1997.

Dockers/Dock Staff
See Stevedores

Drapers

BOYD, PERCIVAL. *Roll of the Draper's Company of London, collected from the Company's records and other sources.* Croydon: J.A. Gordon, 1934. Alphabetical list of members.

BOYD, P. 'Drapers Company of London', *Genealogists' magazine* **5**, 1929-31, 174-5. Primarily concerned with membership records.

GIRTIN, TOM. *The triple crowns: a narrative history of the Drapers Company, 1364-1964.* Hutchinson, 1964. General history.

JOHNSON, A.H. *The history of the Worshipful Company of the Drapers of London.* 5 vols. Oxford: Clarendon Press, 1914-22. Gives many extracts from original sources, including various accounts, tax lists (e.g. 1641 poll tax), lists of officers and members, *etc.*

Drovers

BURNBY, J. *Drovers and tanners of Enfield and Edmonton.* Occasional paper N.S. **51**. E.H.H.S., 1988. Includes some biographical information.

Dyers

DAYNES, JOHN NORMAN. *A short history of the Ancient Mistery of the Dyers of the City of London.* Worshipful Company of Dyers, 1965. Includes various lists of dyers; also pedigree of Tyrwhitt, 12-16th c.

ROBINS, EDWARD COOKWORTHY. 'Some account of the history and antiquities of the Worshipful Company of Dyers, London', *T.L.M.A.S.* **5**, 1881, 441-76. Includes list of prime and renter wardens.

WEBB, CLIFF. *London livery company apprenticeship registers. Volume 25. Dyers Company, 1706-1746.* Society of Genealogists, 1999.

East India Men

BAXTER, I.A. 'Records of the Poplar Pension Fund', *East London record* **8**, 1985, 30-33. Discusses records of pensioners of the East India Company, 19th c. Their almshouse/hospital was at Poplar.

BAXTER, I.A. 'The Poplar Pension Fund', *C.A.* **27**, 1985, 14-17.

Embroiderers

FITCH, MARC. 'The London makers of opus Anglicanum', *T.L.M.A.S.* **27**, 1976, 288-96. Embroiderers, medieval.

Engravers

HEAL, AMBROSE. 'The trade-cards of engravers', *The Print-collectors quarterly* **14**(3), 1927, 219-50. Includes list of engravers, 18-19th c., with brief biographical information.
See also Lawyers. Lincolns Inn

Entomologists

NEAVE, S.A., & GRIFFIN, F.J. *The history of the Entomological Society of London, 1833-1933.* The Society, 1933. Includes list of fellows.

Exchequer Clerks

MILNE, FRANK. 'Some Exchequer officials in the XVIIIth century', *H.C.M.* **3**, 1901, 276-81. Lists of clerks.

Fan Makers

COLLINS, BERNARD ROSS. *A short account of the Worshipful Company of Fan Makers.* Favil Press, 1950. Includes list of masters and wardens, 1709-1948, *etc.*

FOWLES, A.W. *The revised history of the Worshipful Company of Fan Makers, 1709-1975.* The Company, 1977. Includes lists of officers.
See also Broderers

Farriers

PRINCE, LESLIE B. *The farrier and his craft: the history of the Worshipful Company of Farriers.* J.A. Allen, 1980. Includes calendar of documents.

ROBSON, LEONARD C.F. *The farriers of London, being an account of the Worshipful Company of Farriers as described in the records of the Company.* The Company, 1949. Includes list of masters, 1673-1949, and clerks, 1613-1649; also extensive extracts from court minute books and audit books, 1719-1889. Many names.

WEBB, CLIFF. *London livery company apprenticeship register. Volume 28. Farriers Company, 1619-1800.* Society of Genealogists, 1999.

Feltmakers

HAWKINS, J.H. *History of the Worshipful Company of the Art or Mistery of Feltmakers of London.* Crowther & Goodman, 1917. General history, with a list of masters and clerks, 1675-1917.

Figurehead Carvers

'Figurehead carvers', *C.A.* **48**, 1990, 22-3. List, 19th c., with addresses.

Fishermen

DEAR, BOB. 'Thames fishing families', *W.M.* **7**(4), 1989, 127-31. Review of sources.

Fishmongers

HASKETT-SMITH, WALTER PARRY. *The Worshipful Company of Fishmongers of the City of London: lists of apprentices and freemen in 1537 and 1600-50.* Privately published, 1916.

TOWSE, J. WRENCH. *Worshipful Company of Fishmongers of London: a short account of portraits, pictures, plate, etc., etc., in the possession of the Company.* William Clowes and Sons, 1907. Includes list of prime wardens, 1700-1906, and honorary freemen, 1750-1906.

Fletchers

OXLEY, JAMES E. *The Fletchers and Longbowstring Makers of London.* Worshipful Company of Fletchers, 1968. Includes list of masters and wardens, *etc.*

Footballers

Arsenal

KELLY, STEPHEN F. *The Highbury encyclopedia: an A-Z of Arsenal F.C.* Edinburgh: Mainstream Publishing, 1994. Includes brief biographies of leading players.

Chelsea

CHESHIRE, SCOTT. *Chelsea: a complete record, 1905-1991.* Derby: Breedon Books, 1991. Includes biographies of football players.

GLANVILL, RICK. *The Chelsea who's who: Chelsea's heroes and zeroes from Abrams to Zola.* Boxtree, 1998. Footballers.

Finchley

WHIDDON, H. *One hundred years of playing the game, 1874-1974: featuring the history of the Finchley Football Club, the beginning of clubs in North London and South Hertfordshire.* Hillside, 1974.

Fulham

TURNER, DENNIS, & WHITE, ALEX. *Fulham: a complete record 1879-1987.* Derby: Breedon Books, 1987. Includes a biographical dictionary of players.

Millwall

LINDSAY, RICHARD. *Millwall: a complete record, 1885-1991.* Derby: Breedon Books Sport, 1991. Includes biographical dictionary.

MURRAY, JAMES. *Milwall: lions of the South.* Indispensible Publications/Millwall F.C., 1988.

Tottenham Hotspur

GOODWIN, BOB. *The Spurs alphabet: a complete who's who of Tottenham Hotspur F.C.* ACL Colour Print & Polar Publishing (U.K.), 1992.

GOODWIN, BOB. *Spurs: a complete record, 1882-1991.* Derby: Breedon Books, 1991. Includes biographical dictionary of footballers.

HAYES, DEAN. *The White Hart Lane encyclopedia: an A-Z of Tottenham Hotspur F.C.* Edinburgh: Mainstream Publishing, 1996.

Founders

HADLEY, GUY. *Citizens and founders: a history of the Worshipful Company of Founders, London, 1365-1975.* Phillimore, 1976. Includes list of masters.

HIBBERT, WILLIAM NEMBHARD. *History of the Worshipful Company of Founders of the City of London.* Privately printed, 1925. General study, some names.

PARSLOE, GUY, ed. *Wardens' accounts of the Worshipful Company of Founders of the City of London, 1497-1681.* Athlone Press, 1964. Many names of members, *etc.*

WEBB, CLIFF. *London livery company apprenticeship registers Volume 21. Founders Company, 1643-1800.* Society of Genealogists, 1998.

WILLIAMS, WILLIAM MEADE. *Annals of the Worshipful Company of Founders of the City of London.* W.H. Boosey & Co., 1867. Mainly extracts from the Company's archives.

Framework Knitters
See Broderers

Freemasons

Antients Domatic Lodge

WELLS, ROY ARTHUR. *Freemasonry in London from 1785.* Lewis Masonic, 1984. Study of Antients Domatic Lodge no. 1977.

Dundee Lodge

HEIRON, ARTHUR. *Ancient freemasonry and the old Dundee Lodge no.18 (no.9, 1755 to 1813) 1722-23 to 1920.* Kenning & Son, 1921. At Wapping; includes lists of officers.

Bank of England Lodge

POPE, STEPHEN A. *The Bank of England Lodge of Masons no. 263: its history and the lifework of its members in promoting the welfare of the craft for the benefit of all mankind, 1788-1931.* Bank of England Lodge, 1932. Includes list of members.

Emulation Lodge

DYER, COLIN F.W. *Emulation: a ritual to remember: notes on the men and times in the history of Emulation Lodge of Improvement, 1823-1973.* A Lewis, for Emulation Lodge of Improvement, 1973. Many freemasons mentioned.

SADLER, HENRY. *History and records of the Lodge of Emulation no. 21 of ancient free and accepted masons of England, 1723-1906.* Warrington & Co., 1906. Many names of freemasons mentioned.

SADLER, HENRY. *Illustrated history of the Emulation Lodge of Improvement no. 256, 1823-1903, with brief historical sketches of its branches and offshoots.* Spencer & Co., 1904. Many names.

Grand Stewards Lodge

CALVERT, ALBERT FREDERICK. *The Grand Stewards Lodge, 1735-1920.* Kenning & Son, 1920. Freemasons; includes list of masters.

CALVERT, ALBERT F. *The Grand Stewards and Red Apron Lodges.* Kenning & Son, 1917. Includes extensive lists of officers, etc.

Lion & Lamb Lodge

HUGHAN, WILLIAM JAMES. *History of the Lion and Lamb Lodge, London, no. 192.* George Kenning, 1894. Includes many names of freemasons.

Old Concord Lodge

CAREY, W.H.B. *History of Old Concord Lodge no. 172, 1764-1967.* The Lodge, 1967. Includes lists of various officers.

Paviors Lodge

BROAD, WALLER. *List of officers and members of Pavior's Lodge no. 5646. and notes about the Lodge.* The Lodge, 1962. Since 1936.

St. James Lodge

REED, W.H. *Masonry in London and Middlesex: being the history of the old St. James's Lodge (1740-1813) and the Royal Union Lodge (1825 to recent times) and comprising much information of interest to masons generally.* Hornsey & Tottenham Press, 1906. Includes many names of freemasons.

Shakespeare Lodge

EBBLEWHITE, ERNEST ARTHUR. *The history of the Shakespeare Lodge no. 99, 1757-1904.* Privately printed, 1905. Includes 'biographical list of members'. Continued by:

STEINTHAL, WILLIAM B.L. *The history of the Shakespeare Lodge no. 99. Supplement, 1905-1939.* Privately printed, 1939.

Westminster & Keystone Lodge

GODDING, J.W. SLEIGH. *A history of the Westminster and Keystone Lodge of ancient free and accepted masons, no. 10, from the date of its constitution, 28 January 1722, to the year 1905.* Plymouth: Wm. Brendon & Son, 1907. Includes various lists of officers and members.

Framework Knitters

See Broderers

Freemen

In the past 300 years, some 300,000 people have become freemen of the City of London. It is therefore well worth checking freeman records. The standard introduction to these records is now:

ALDOUS, VIVIENNE E. *My ancestors were freemen of the City of London.* Society of Genealogists, 1999.

See also:

ALDOUS, VIVIENNE. *City freedom archives at the Corporation of London Records Office.* Rev. ed. Research guide 1. Corporation of London, 1996.

ALDOUS, VIVIENNE E. 'The archives of the Freedom of the City of London', *Genealogists magazine* 23(4), 1989, 128-33. Freemen of the City of London are listed — inaccurately — in:

WELCH, CHARLES. *Register of freemen of the City of London in the reign of Henry VIII and Edward VI.* London and Middlesex Archaeological Society, 1908. This volume is incomplete and not to be trusted — but should, nevertheless, be consulted by everyone seeking mid-16th century London ancestors. For a review, see:

MARSH, BOWER. 'A London manuscript', *Genealogist* N.S. 32, 1916, 217-20.

Other works on London's freemen include:

SALISBURY, EDWARD. 'List of liverymen and freemen of the city companies, A.D. 1538', *M.H.N.Q.* 3, 1897, 39-43, 80-82, 151-4 & 187-91; 4, 1898, 17-21 & 68-9.

WHITEBROOK, J.C., ed. *London citizens in 1651, being a transcript of Harleian ms.4778.* Hutchins & Romer, 1910. Lists freemen of 22 companies; also includes jury list, 1661.

MEDLYCOTT, MERVYN T. 'The City of London freedom registers', *Genealogists magazine* **19**(2), 1977, 45-7. Also published in *N.M.* **3**(3), 1981, 43-6.

RAMSAY, G.D. 'The recruitment and fortunes of some London freemen in the mid-sixteenth century', *Economic History Review* 2nd series **31**, 1978, 526-40. General discussion.

London's roll of fame, being complimentary notes and addresses from the City of London on presentation of the Honorary Freedom of that City, and on other occasions ... from the close of the reign of George II, A.D. 1757 to 1884. Cassell & Co., 1884.

London's roll of fame, being records of presentations of the freedom of the city and addresses of welcome from the Corporation of London to royal and other distinguished personages, A.D. 1885-1959. Corporation of London, [1959].

DYER, COLIN. *The Guild of Freemen of the City of London: a record of its formation and history.* The Guild, 1982. Includes list of officers, 20th c., with biographical notes on masters.

Fruiterers

GOULD, ARTHUR WILLIAM. *History of the Worshipful Company of Fruiterers of the City of London.* Exeter: William Pollard & Co., 1911. Includes lists of members, 16-20th c., some with addresses.
See also Broderers

Fullers

See Cloth Workers

Furniture Makers

HEAL, SIR AMBROSE. *The London furniture makers, from the Restoration to the Victorian era, 1660-1840: a record of 2,500 cabinet makers, upholsterers, carvers and gilders, with their addresses and working dates ...* B.T. Batsford, 1953. Supplemented by:

AGIUS, PAULINE. 'Cabinet-makers not in "Heal": eighteenth and nineteenth-century trade cards of furniture makers in the John Johnson collection of printed ephemera', *Furniture history: the journal of the Furniture History Society* **10**, 1974, 82-4.

FORMAN, BENNO M. 'Continental furniture craftsmen in London, 1511-1625', *Furniture history: the journal of the Furniture History Society* **7**, 1971, 94-120. Lists 400 craftsmen.

MASSIL, WILLIAM I. *Immigrant furniture workers in London, 1881-1939, and the Jewish contribution to the furniture trade.* Jewish Museum, 1997. Includes list of immigrant furniture workers.

KIRKHAM, PAT. *The London furniture trade, 1700-1870.* Furniture History Society, 1988. Scholarly study, many names. Also issued as *Furniture history* **24**, 1988.

OLIVER, J. LEONARD. 'The East London furniture industry', *East London papers* **4**(2), 1961, 88-101. Discussion of the value of 19th c. trade directories as evidence.

PINTO, EDWARD H. *The origins and history of the Worshipful Company of Furniture Makers.* The Company, 1964. Includes list of office bearers and liverymen in 1964.

Gardeners

BARNES, MELVYN. *Root and branch: a history of the Worshipful Company of Gardeners of London.* The Company, 1994. Includes various lists of names.

CROSWELLER, WILLIAM THOMAS. *The Gardeners Company: a short chronological history, 1605-1907.* Blades, East and Blades, 1908. Many names, but no index.

STEELE, ARNOLD FRANCIS. *The Worshipful Company of Gardeners of London: a history of its revival, 1890-1960.* The Company, 1964. Includes lists of officers from 1605.

WELCH, CHARLES. *History of the Worshipful Company of Gardeners.* 2nd ed. Blades, East and Blades, 1900. Includes 'A list of the master, wardens, court of assistants, livery and freemen of the Worshipful Company of Gardeners, 1900-1901.'
See also Broderers

Geologists

WOODWARD, HORACE B.BOLINGBROKE. *The history of the Geological Society of London.* Geological Society, 1907. Includes lists of officers, benefactors, medallists, *etc.*

Girdlers

BARKER, T.C. *The Girdler's Company: a second history.* The Company, 1957. Includes list of masters.

SMYTHE, W. DUMVILLE. *An historical account of the Worshipful Company of Girdlers, London.* Chiswick Press, 1905. Includes list of masters, 12-20th c.

Glass Makers & Sellers

BONE, GEORGE ALLAN. *The Worshipful Company of Glass Sellers of London from its inception to the present day.* [The Company], 1966. Includes a few brief biographies, and lists of officers from 1664.

BUCKLEY, FRANCIS. *Old London glasshouses.* Stevens & Sons, 1915. Many glass makers named.

HOWARD, ALEXANDER L. *The Worshipful Company of Glass-Sellers of London, from its inception to the present day.* Glass-Sellers Company, [1940]. Includes many extracts from minute books, with a list of masters and wardens, 1664-1940.

RAMSEY, WILLIAM. *The Worshipful Company of Glass Sellers of London.* The Company, 1898. Includes list of the livery in 1898, *etc.*

WEBB, CLIFF. *London livery companies apprenticeship registers volume 5. Glass-sellers Company 1664-1812; Woolmens Company 1665-1828.* Society of Genealogists, 1997.

YOUNG, SIDNEY. *The history of the Worshipful Company of Glass Sellers of London.* Geo. Barber, 1913. Includes biographical notes on prominent members.

Glaziers

ASHDOWN, CHARLES HENRY. *History of the Worshipful Company of Glaziers of the City of London, otherwise the Company of Glaziers and Painters of Glass.* Blades, East and Blades, 1919. Includes list of masters and wardens, 1328-1918, list of the Company's archives, *etc.*

WEBB, CLIFF. *London livery companies apprenticeship registers volume 7. Glaziers Company, 1694-1800.* Society of Genealogists, 1997.

Glovers

WEBB, CLIFF. *London livery companies apprenticeship registers Volume 4. Glovers Company 1675-79, 1735-48, 1766-1804.* Society of Genealogists, 1996.

Gold & Silver Wyre Drawers

WEBB, CLIFF. *London livery company apprenticeship registers volume 15. Gold and Silver Wyre Drawers Company, 1693-1837.* Society of Genealogists, 1998.

A list of the master, wardens, court of assistants and livery of the Worshipful Company of Gold and Silver Wyre Drawers of the City of London, with a short history of the craft it represents. Chiswick Press, 1922. Other editions also available.

Goldsmiths

BUCKLEY, FRANCIS. *Old London goldsmiths 1666-1706 recorded in the newspapers.* Uppermill: Moore & Edwards, 1926.

CAMPBELL, MARIAN. 'English goldsmiths in the fifteenth century', in WILLIAMS, DANIEL, ed. *England in the fifteenth century: proceedings of the 1986 Harlaxton symposium.* Woodbridge: Boydell Press, 1987, 43-52. Brief discussion of who they were and what they did.

CHAFFERS, WILLIAM. *Gilda aurifabrorum: a history of English goldsmiths and plateworkers and their works stamped on plate copied in fac-simile from celebrated examples, and the earliest examples preserved at Goldsmiths Hall, London, with their names, addresses and dates of entry ...* W.H. Allen & Co., 1883.

CULME, JOHN. *The directory of London gold and silversmiths, jewellers, and allied traders, 1838-1914, from the London Assay Office registers.* 2 vols. Woodbridge: Antique Collectors Club, 1987. 4000 biographies.

EVANS, JOAN. 'Huguenot goldsmiths of London', *Pr.Hug.Soc.L.* **15**, 1934-7, 516-20. List.

FALLON, JOHN P. *Marks of London goldsmiths and silversmiths (c.1697-1837)*. New ed. Newton Abbot: David & Charles, 1988. Effectively a biographical dictionary.

GRIMWADE, ARTHUR G. *London goldsmiths, 1697-1837: their marks and lives*. 3rd ed. Faber & Faber, 1990. Extensive listing.

HARE, SUSAN M. 'The records of the Goldsmiths' Company', *Archives* **16**(72), 1984, 376-84. Includes a list of records relating to both members and properties.

HEAL, AMBROSE, SIR. *The London goldsmiths, 1200-1800: a record of the names and addresses of the craftsmen, their shop-signs and trade-cards*. Cambridge University Press, 1935. Reprinted Newton Abbot: David & Charles, 1972.

KENT, TIMOTHY ARTHUR. 'Salisbury goldsmiths and London wardens, 1631-7', *Hatcher review* **2**(15), 1983, 208-17. Includes brief list with biographical notes.

MITCHELL, DAVID, ed. *Goldsmiths, silversmiths and bankers: innovation and the transfer of skill, 1550 to 1750*. Centre for Metropolitan History working papers series 2. Stroud: Alan Sutton, 1995. Collection of essays.

PRICE, FREDERICK GEORGE. *Some account of Lombard Street, its early goldsmiths, and the signs of their houses*. Institute of Bankers, 1886. Includes list of goldsmiths resident in the parish of St.Mary Woolnoth, 1434-1729; also list of signs with names of occupants.

PRICE, F.G. HILTON. 'Some notes on the early goldsmiths and bankers, to the close of the seventeenth century', *T.L.M.A.S.* **5**, 1881, 235-81. Includes brief biographical notes.

PRIDEAUX, WALTER TREVERBIAN. *A list of the wardens, members of the Court of Assistants, and liverymen of the Worshipful Company of Goldsmiths, since 1688*. Arden Press, 1936.

PRIDEAUX, SIR WALTER SHERBURNE. *Memorials of the Goldsmiths Company, being gleanings from their records between the years 1335 and 1815*. 2 vols. Eyre & Spottiswoode, 1896. Includes many names.

REDDAWAY, T.F. *The early history of the Goldsmiths Company, 1327-1509*. Edward Arnold, 1975. Includes WALKER, LORNA E.M. *The book of ordinances, 1478-83*, with biographical notices of those mentioned in it; also includes lists of officers.

STAPLES, JOHN. 'Members of the Goldsmiths Company who have been aldermen of the Ward of Aldersgate', *T.L.M.A.S.* **7**(1), 1888 [also referred to as **6**, 1890, appendix], 1-35.

Grocers

BARNES, L. HICKMAN, & ELLISON-MACCARTNEY, J. *A short history of the Grocers Company ...* Metcalfe & Cooper, 1950. Includes brief note on records.

GRANTHAM, W.W. *List of the Wardens of the Grocers Company from 1345 to 1907 ...* [Privately published], 1907.

HEATH, J.B. *Some account of the Worshipful Company of Grocers of the City of London*. 3rd ed. Privately printed, 1869. Includes extensive 'notices of eminent members'.

KINGDON, JOHN ABERNETHY. *Facsimile of the first volume of ms. archives of the Worshipful Company of Grocers, A.D. 1345-1463*. 2 vols. The Company, 1883-6. Extensive account book, recording many names, but unfortunately without an index.

REES, J. AUBREY. *The Worshipful Company of Grocers: an historical retrospect, 1345-1923*. Chapman and Dodd, 1923. General account, but little for the genealogist.

The Grocers Company, 1345-1920. The Company, [1920?] Includes list of honorary freemen from 1660.

Grocers Hall and the principal objects of interest therein. [Grocers Company], 1936. Includes names of some early members; also a few notes on masters.

List of the wardens of the Grocers' Company from 1345 to 1907, taken from the ordinances, remembrances and wardens' accounts, 1345-1463 ...; the quires of wardens' accounts, 1454-1750; the register of freemen and apprentices, 1447-1504; the minute books of the Company, 1556-1907. Metcalfe & Cooper, 1907.

29

Gunmakers

BLACKMORE, HOWARD L. *A dictionary of London gunmakers, 1350-1850.* Oxford: Phaidon, 1986. Extensive listing, with useful 'notes on sources'.

HAYWARD, J.F. 'The Huguenot gunmakers of London', *Pr.Hug.Soc.L.* **20**(6), 1966, 649-63. Includes list with biographical notes.

HOLLAENDER, A.E.J. 'The archives of the Worshipful Company of Gunmakers of the City of London', *Archives* **1**(8), 1952, 8-19.

WEBB, CLIFF. *London livery companies apprenticeship registers volume 8. Gunmakers Company, 1656-1800.* Society of Genealogists, 1997.

Haberdashers

ARCHER, IAN W. *The history of the Haberdashers' Company.* Chichester: Phillimore, 1992. Detailed history, including lists of masters and wardens, 1582-1990, and of clerks; also useful listing of company records.

PREVETT, HARRY. *A short description of the Worshipful Company of Haberdashers.* The Company, 1971. Includes lists of masters and clerks, 16-20th c.

The Worshipful Company of Haberdashers: the descriptive class list of records. The Company, 1954. Typescript.

Hackney Coach Drivers

A list of the 400 Hackney Coaches licensed in July and August 1662 by the Commission appointed by the King's Majesties Commission ... together with their names, places of abode and figure marks. [ ], 1664.

Heralds

CHESSYRE, HERBERT, & AILES, ADRIAN. *Heralds of today: a biographical list of the officers of the College of Arms, London, 1963-86.* Gerrards Cross: Van Duren, 1986.

NICKELLS, JANE. 'The ghosts of the College of Arms', *Coat of Arms* N.S. **8**(152), 1990, 306-14. Brief biographical notes on heralds; includes list of officers, staff and families buried at St.Benet, Paul's Wharf. 1620-1837.

Hockey Players

HOWELLS, M.K. *A centenary of modern hockey 1871-1971: a brief history centred round the Teddington Hockey Club.* The author, 1971. Includes some names of players.

Horners

FISHER, F.J. *A short history of the Worshipful Company of Horners.* Croydon: George Becker, 1936. Includes various lists of names, and a few probate inventories.
See also Broderers

Horse Breeders

HEWLETT, GEOFFREY. 'The worthy gentlemen of Kingsbury', *Wembley History Society journal* **5**(1), 1980, 1-4; **5**(2), 1981, 34-40. Notes on horse breeders and trainers, late 19th-early 20th c.

Horticulturalists
See Nurserymen

Innkeepers

BERRY, GEORGE. *Taverns and tokens of Pepys' London.* Seaby Publications, 1978. Includes list of innkeepers mentioned by Pepys the diarist.

ROGERS, KENNETH. *Signs & taverns round about Old London Bridge (including Gracechurch Street, Fenchurch Street & Leadenhall Street.)* Homeland Association, 1937. Includes many names of innkeepers etc.

WARNER, OLIVER. *A history of the Innholders Company.* S. Straker & Sons, 1962. Includes list of masters, 1653-1961, etc.

History of the Worshipful Company of Innholders of the City of London. Bemrose & Sons, 1922. Mentions many names, but lacks an index.

WEBB, CLIFF. *London livery company apprenticeship registers, volume 17. Innholders Company, 1642-1643, 1654-1670, 1673-1800.* Society of Genealogists, 1998.

'The taverns in Middlesex and Hertfordshire', *M.H.N.Q.* **4**, 1898, 76-80, 137-8 & 203-4. Lists innkeepers.

Acton

HARPER SMITH, T., & A. *Acton inns & pubs.* Acton past & present **18**. Acton History Group, 1989. Gives many names of innkeepers.

Bishopsgate

GOSS, C.W.F. 'The White Hart, Bishopsgate', *T.L.M.A.S.* N.S. **6**, 1933, 257-83. Traces innkeepers.

Ruislip

COY, COLLEEN A. 'Good pub guide, 1851-1881', *R.N.E.* April 1989, 1-6. Lists innkeepers from the censuses, 1851-81, and the rate book, 1863.

Staines

PEARSE, E.A. 'Staines inns, 1650-1730', *Staines Local History Society journal* **2**, 1967, 10-21. Includes list of victuallers licences granted, 1730.

Sunbury

HESELTON, KEN. 'Lost pubs of Sunbury', *J.S.S.L.H.S.* **20**, 1988, 10-12; **23**, 1989, 12-13; **24**, 1990, 8-10; **26**, 1991, 6-9. Includes names of innkeepers.

Instrument Makers

BROWN, JOYCE. *Mathematical instrument makers in the Grocers Company, 1688-1800: with notes on some earlier makers.* Science Museum, 1979.

CRAWFORTH, M.A. 'Instrument makers in the London guilds', *Annals of science* **44**, 1987, 319-77. Includes some biographical notes on 72 instrument makers, 17-19th c., with a list of masters and apprentices in the Joiners Company.

Insurance Policy Holders

TRIMBLE, NAN. 'Sun Insurance policy registers: entries for Sunbury, 1715/16-1775', *J.S.S.L.H.S.* **25**, 1990, 12-13. Names policy holders.

WULCKO, LAURENCE M. 'Fire insurance policies as a source of local history', *Local historian* **9**, 1970, 3-8. Deals mainly with London.

Insurers

List of subscribers to Lloyds from the foundation in 1771 to the first of June 1810. William Phillips, 1810.

Ironmongers

GLOVER, ELIZABETH. *A history of the Ironmongers Company.* Worshipful Company of Ironmongers, 1991. Includes lists of masters and beadles from the 15th c.

HERBERT, WILLIAM. *History of the Worshipful Company of Ironmongers of London, principally compiled from their own records.* J. & C. Adlard, 1837. Re-issue of a section of his *History of the twelve great livery companies of London.* Includes notes on trust estates and charities.

NICHOLL, JOHN. *Some account of the Worshipful Company of Ironmongers.* 2nd ed. Privately printed, 1866. Includes notes on miscellaneous benefactions, list of masters, extracts from records, *etc.*

NOBLE, T.C. *A brief history of the Worshipful Company of Ironmongers, London, A.D. 1351-1889, with an appendix containing some account of the Blacksmiths Company.* Spottiswoode & Co., 1889. Includes biographical notes on charitable ironmongers.

WEBB, CLIFF. *London livery company apprenticeship registers, volume 24. Ironmongers Company, 1655-1800.* Society of Genealogists, 1999.

Jewellers

See Goldsmiths

Joiners

PHILLIPS, HENRY LAVEROCK. *Annals of the Worshipful Company of Joiners of the City of London, extracted from original documents, minute books, and renter wardens' accounts, etc., from A.D. 1237-1850, together with a chronological list of the feoffees of the Company from A.D. 1497-1885, and an alphabetical list of the livery from A.D. 1496-1914, with the dates of their livery.* Privately printed, 1915.

See also Instument Makers

Launderers

HARPER SMITH, T., & A. *Soapsud Island: Acton laundries.* Acton past & present **14**. Acton History Group, 1988. Includes many names of launderers.

MALCOLMSON, PATRICIA E. 'Laundresses and the laundry trade in Victorian England', *Victorian studies* **24**, 1980-81, 439-62. General discussion.

Lawyers

HORWITZ, HENRY, & BONFIELD, LLOYD. 'The lower branches of the legal profession: a London Society of attorneys and solicitors of the 1730, and its moots', *Cambridge law journal* **49**, 1990, 461-90. Includes list of 24 members, with biographical notes.

PARMITER, GEOFFREY DEC. *Elizabethan Popish recusancy in the Inns of Court.* Bulletin of the Institute of Historical Research special supplement **11**. 1976. General study; many names.

SHERR, MERRILL F. 'Religion and the legal profession: a study of the religious sensibilities of 16th century London lawyers', *Historical magazine of the Protestant Episcopal Church* **45**, 1976, 211-24. Includes a list of lawyers and their religious affiliations, 16th c.

Barnards Inn

ROUTLEDGE, R.A. 'The records of Barnard's Inn: an archival adventure', *Journal of legal history* **1**, 1980, 65-74. Description of surviving records — including admission registers, 1620-1869.

Clements Inn

CARR, CECIL, SIR. ed. *Pension book of Clement's Inn.* Publications of the Selden Society **78**, 1960. Includes list of members, with their sureties, 1658-1883.

Furnivals Inn

BLAND, D.S., ed. *Early records of Furnivals Inn, edited from a Middle Temple manuscript.* Newcastle upon Tyne: Kings College, Dept of Extra Mural Studies, 1957. Extracts from accounts, minutes, *etc.,* with some names of members.

Grays Inn

FLETCHER, REGINALD J., ed. *The pension book of Gray's Inn (records of the honourable society), 1569-[1800].* 2 vols. Chiswick Press, 1901-10. Includes many names, with a list of treasurers, 1530-1909, and list of occupants of Grays Inn, 1668.

FOSTER, JOSEPH. *The register of admissions to Grays Inn, 1521-1889, together with the register of marriages in Gray's Inn Chapel, 1695-1754.* Hansard Publishing Union, 1889.
See also Soldiers

Inner Temple

COOKE, W.H., ed. *Students admitted to the Inner Temple, 1547-1660.* William Clowes & Sons, 1877.

INDERWICK, F.A., & ROBERTS, R.A., eds. *A calendar of the Inner Temple records.* 5 vols. Henry Sotheran & Co., *et al,* 1896-1937. Includes subsidy roll, 1523, for the Inns of Court, Chancery, and officers of the courts of law, together with a register of burials in the Inner Temple, 1628-60. Also includes many other names.

LAMB, CHARLES. *The old benchers of the Inner Temple,* with annotations by Sir F.D. Mackinnon. Oxford: Clarendon Press, 1927. Includes brief biographies of prominent lawyers.

WILLIAMSON, JOHN BRUCE. *The history of the Temple, London, from the institution of the order of the Knights of the Temple to the close of the Stuart period, compiled from the original records of the two learned and Honourable Societies of the Temple.* 2nd ed. John Murray, 1925. History of two Inns of Court, ie. the Inner Temple and the Middle Temple.

Masters of the Bench of the Hon. Society of the Inner Temple, 1450-1883, and masters of the Temple, 1540-1883. William Clowes and Sons, 1883. There are two supplements:

Masters of the Bench of the Hon.Society of the Inner Temple. Supplement, 1888-1900, to which is appended a list of the treasurers, 1505-1901. C. Whittingham and Co., 1901.

Masters of the Bench of the Hon. Society of the Inner Temple. Second supplement, 1901-1918, with addenda to the previous supplement; a list of the treasurers, 1901-18; masters of the Temple from 1894; an index to both supplements. [ ], 1918.

See also Soldiers, Militiamen, *etc.*

Inns of Court

COKAYNE, G.E. 'Admissions to the Inns of Court, London', *Genealogist* N.S. **15**, 1899, 71-5.

BLAND, D.S. *A bibliography of the Inns of Court and Chancery.* Supplementary series **3**. Selden Society, 1965.

See also Soldiers, Militiamen, *etc.,* and under the various inns

Law Society

The records of the Society of Gentlemen Practisers in the courts of law and equity, called the Law Society. Incorporated Law Society, 1897. Abstracts of original documents, 18-19th c., with many names of lawyers.

Lincolns Inn

BAILDON, W. PAILEY. *Records of the Honourable Society of Lincolns Inn: admissions, 1420-1893, and chapel registers.* 2 vols. Lincolns Inn, 1896.

BAILDON, W.P., ed. *The records of the Society of Lincoln's Inn: the black books.* 4 vols. H.S. Cartwright for the Society, 1897-1902. Includes many names, with notes on heraldry, list of calls to the bar, and of painters and engravers, *etc.*

Middle Temple

BEDWELL, C.E.A. 'American Middle Templars', *American historical review* **25**, 1919-20, 680-89. List, 1681-1836.

HUTCHINSON, JOHN. *A catalogue of notable Middle Templars, with brief biographical notices.* Butterworth, 1902.

INGPEN, ARTHUR ROBERT. *The Middle Temple bench books, being a register of benchers of the Middle Temple from the earliest records to the present time, with historical introduction.* Chiswick Press, 1912. Includes list of treasurers, masters, readers, *etc.,* with brief biographical notes.

STURGESS, H.A.C. *Register of admissions to the Honourable Society of the Middle Temple, from the fifteenth century to the year 1944.* Butterworth, for the Society, 1949.

MARTIN, CHARLES TRICE, ed. *Middle Temple records.* 4 vols. Butterworth, 1904-5. Minutes of Parliament, 1501-1703. Includes many names.

WILLIAMSON, J. BRUCE. *The Middle Temple bench book: being a register of benchers of the Middle Temple from the earliest records to the present time, with historical introduction.* 2nd ed. Chancery Lane Press, 1937. Includes various lists of officers.

WILLIAMSON, J.BRUCE. *Roll of honour, including the names of all who are commemorated in the windows of the Hall of the Honble. Society of the Middle Temple.* The Middle Temple, 1925. Memorials to prominent members of the Temple since medieval times.

See also Inner Temple

Serjeants Inn

KING, H.C. *Records and documents concerning Serjeants Inn, Fleet Street.* Richard Flint & Co., 1922. Includes wills, accounts, deeds, brief lists of tenants, 1806 and 1820, *etc.*

Solicitors Company

STEELE, ARNOLD F. *The Worshipful Company of Solicitors of the City of London: a commentary on the Company's surviving records.* The Company, [1968]. Includes list of surviving records (from 1908) and many 20th c. names.

Staple Inn

WILLIAMS, E. *Staple Inn: customs' house, wool court, and inn of Chancery.* Archibald Constable, 1906. Includes list of admissions, 1716-1881, list of members, 1585, *etc.*

Law Firms

SCOTT, JOHN. *Legibus: a history of Clifford-Turner, 1900-80.* Hove: King, Thorne & Stace, 1980. Includes list of London partners; also pedigrees of Turner and Vachell, 18-20th c.

SLINN, JUDY. *A history of Freshfields.* Freshfields, 1984. City solicitors; includes much information on the Freshfield family, also list of partners, 1716-1983.

SLINN, JUDY. *Linklaters & Paines: the first one hundred and fifty years.* Longman, 1987. City solicitors; includes list of partners with brief biographical notes; also lists of long-serving staff.

Leathersellers
BLACK, WILLIAM HENRY. *History and antiquities of the Worshipful Company of Leathersellers, of the City of London, with fac-similes of charters ...* E.J. Francis, 1871. Includes list of masters, and many extracts from original sources.

Librarians
HARRIS, P.R. *A history of the British Museum library, 1753-1953.* British Library, 1998. Includes list of senior staff, also list of 'some holders of readers' tickets, 1759-1939'.

Lieutenants etc., of the Tower
NICHOLS, JOHN GOUGH. 'The lieutenants of the Tower of London', *T.L.M.A.S.* **1**, 1860, 225-42. Includes biographical notes, 16th c.
RUTTON, WILLIAM LOFTIE. 'Constables and Lieutenants of the Tower', *Notes and queries* 10th series **9**, 1908, 61-3, 161-3, 243-6 & 490-1. See also 390-91 & 490-91, & **10**, 1908, 70-72, 118, 213-4 & 277. List with brief notes.

Local Government Officers
CLIFTON, GLORIA C. *Professionalism, patronage and public service in Victorian London: the staff of the Metropolitan Board of Works, 1856-1889.* Athlone Press, 1992. Includes lists of Board members and chief officers, *etc.,* with extensive bibliography.
MASTERS, BETTY R. *The Chamberlain of the City of London, 1237-1987.* Corporation of London, 1988. Detailed history; includes list.
MASTERS, BETTY R. 'The City Surveyor, the City Engineer, the City Architect and Planning Officer', *Gl.M.* **4**(4), 1973, 237-55. Includes lists.
MASTERS, BETTY R. 'City officers, I: the Common Serjeant', *Gl.M.* **2**(9), 1967, 379-89. Includes list.
Recorders of the City of London 1289-1850. Court of Aldermen, [1850]. List.

MASTERS, BETTY R. 'City officers, II: the Secondary', *Gl.M.* **2**(10), 1968, 425-33. List, 15-20th c. The secondaries were officers of the sheriff.
MASTERS, BETTY R. 'City officers, III: the Town Clerk', *Gl.M.* **3**(1), 1969, 55-74. Includes list.

Longbowstring Makers
See Fletchers

Looking Glass Makers
WILLS, GEOFFREY. *English looking-glasses: a study of the glass, frames and makers (1670-1820).* Country Life, 1965. Includes 'A directory of London makers and sellers of looking-glasses'.

Lords Lieutenants
PACKETT, C. NEVILLE. *Her Majesty's Commission of Lieutenancy for the City of London: a brief history.* [ ], 1987.

Loriners
See Spectacle Makers

Maltmen
PAM, D.O. *Tudor Enfield: the maltmen and the Lea Navigation.* Occasional paper N.S. **18**. E.H.H.S., [1970]. Includes list of maltmen accused of offences on the River Lea.

Map Sellers
TYACKE, SARAH. *London map-sellers, 1660-1720: a collection of advertisements for maps placed in the London Gazette, 1668-1719, with biographical notes on the map-sellers.* Tring: Map Collector Publications, 1978.

Market Gardeners
See Nurserymen

Martyrs
CHAUNCY, MAURICE. *The passion and martyrdom of the holy Carthusian fathers: the short narration.* ed. G.W.S. Curtis. S.P.C.K. for the Church Historical Society, 1935. Desciption of the sufferings of 18 Catholic martyrs, mainly from the London Charterhouse.

TYBURN NUNS. *They died at Tyburn.* Tyburn Convent, 1961. Includes list of Roman Catholic martyrs, 1535-1681.

Masons

CONDER, EDWARD. *Records of the hole crafte and fellowship of masons, with a chronicle of the history of the Worshipful Company of Masons of the City of London.* Swan Sonnenschein & Co., 1894. Includes list of masters and wardens, 1620-1894, *etc.*

HARVEY, JOHN. 'The masons of Westminster Abbey', *Archaeological journal* 113, 1956, 82-101. Includes list, 1341-1534.

KNOOP, DOUGLAS, & JONES, G.P. *The London mason in the seventeenth century.* Manchester: Manchester University Press, 1935. Also published in *Ars Quatuor Coronatorum* 48(1), 1935. Includes lists from various sources.

KNOOP, D., & JONES, G.P. 'London Bridge and its builders: a study of the municipal employment of masons in the fifteenth century', *Ars Quatuor Coronatorum* 47, 1934, 5-44. General study of masons.

SMITH, RAYMOND. *The Worshipful Company of Masons.* [The Company], 1960. Includes lists of masters and clerks, 17-20th c.

WEBB, CLIFF. *London livery company apprenticeship registers, Volume 27. Masons Company, 1663-1805.* Society of Genealogists, 1999.

Mayors, Sheriffs, Aldermen and Councillors

For aldermen, there are two important listings:

BEAVEN, ALFRED B. *Aldermen of the City of London temp Henry III – 1908, with notes on the parliamentary representation of the City, the Aldermen and the livery companies, the aldermanic veto, aldermanic baronets and knights, etc.* 2 vols. Corporation of the City of London, 1908-13.

WOODHEAD, J.R. *The rulers of London 1660-1689: a biographical record of the aldermen and common councilmen of the City of London.* London and Middlesex Archaeological Society, 1965. Biographical dictionary.

See also:

Woodcock's lives of illustrious Lords Mayors and aldermen of London, with a brief history of the City of London, also a chronological list of the lords mayors and sheriffs of London and Middlesex from the earliest period to the present time. Alex Dangerfield & Effingham Willson, [1846].

CHANCELLOR, WILLIAM. *Account of the several wards, precincts and parishes in the City of London, to which are added lists of lord-mayors, aldermen, sheriffs, recorders, chamberlains, comptrollers, town clerks and other officers from 1660 to the present time.* Rev. ed. by G. Kearsley. The Reviser, 1787.

OWL. 'An early list of aldermen', *Genealogist* N.S. 4, 1887, 116. See also 175-6. 13th c.

ELLIOT, DAVID C. 'Elections to the Common Council of the City of London, December 21, 1659', *G.S.L.H.* 4, 1979-81, 151-201. Includes list of the 231 Common Council men for 1660, plus other lists.

A return of the number of electors in each ward of the City of London, and of the number of aldermen and common councilmen elected by each ward, and their occupations. House of Commons Parliamentary paper, 1865, XLIV, 555-61. Names, addresses and occupations of aldermen and common councilmen.

Return of the number of electors in each ward of the City of London, and of the number of aldermen and common councilmen elected by each ward, and their occupations and addresses ... House of Commons Parliamentary papers, 1882, LII, 361-9. Gives names, addresses and occupations of aldermen and common councilmen.

A number of works list mayors, sheriffs, etc. of the Corporation:

HOPE, VALERIE. *My Lord Mayor: eight hundred years of London's mayoralty.* Weidenfeld & Nicolson, 1989. Includes list of lord mayors.

MILFORD, ANNA. *Lord mayors of London.* West Wickham: Comerford and Miller, 1989. Popular account; includes list and brief biographical notes.

35

ORRIDGE, B.B. *Some account of the citizens of London and their rulers from 1060 to 1867, and a calendar of the mayors and sheriffs from 1189 to 1867.* Effingham Wilson, 1867.

City biography: containing anecdotes and memoirs of the rise, progress, situation & character of the aldermen and other conspicuous personages of the Corporation and City of London. 2nd ed. The author [anon], 1800.

Lives of illustrious lords mayors and aldermen of London, from the earliest to the present time. Alex Dangerfield & Co., [1845]. Lives of some of the most prominent figures only.

'Lord mayors and sheriffs, temp James I', in PHILLIMORE, W.P.W., ed. *The London & Middlesex notebook.* Elliot Stock, 1892, 51-62, 99-109, 154-65, 201-9 & 252-68. Not completed.

COKAYNE, G.E. *Some account of the Lord Mayors and sheriffs of the City of London during the first quarter of the seventeenth century, 1601 to 1625.* Phillimore & Co., 1897. Chronological; brief biographies.

COKAYNE, G.E. 'Some account of some of the Lord Mayors and Sheriffs of London during the sixteenth century', *T.L.M.A.S.* N.S. 1, 1905, 177-82. Not continued. Solely concerned with descents of the Leveson and Calthorpe families, 16th c.

See also Actors. Dramatic records

Medical Professions

BLOOM, J. HARVEY, & JAMES, R. RUTSON. *Medical practitioners in the Diocese of London under the act of 3 Henry VIII, c.II: an annotated list, 1529-1725.* Cambridge: C.U.P., 1935.

COOK, HAROLD J. *The decline of the old medical regime in Stuart London.* Ithaca: Cornell University Press, 1986. Detailed history; includes useful bibliography.

PETERSON, M. JEANNE. *The medical profession in mid-Victorian London.* Berkeley: University of California Press, 1978. Includes useful notes on sources.

ROBERTS, R.S. 'The personnel and practice of medicine in Tudor and Stuart England, part 2: London', *Medical history* 8, 1964, 217-34. General discussion.

WYMAN, A.L. 'Fulham doctors of the past', *Medical history* 16, 1972, 254-65.

'A catalogue of such Popish physicians in and about the City of London as the author either knoweth, or by good information heareth of', *Catholic ancestor* 4(3), 1992, 111-12. List drawn up c. 1624.

Kellys London medical directory, 7 issues. Kelly & Co., 1889-95. 'The districts contained in the directory extend from Hounslow West to Barking East, and from Croydon South to Barnet North' − title page of 7th ed. Lists many allied professions e.g. coroners, surgical instrument makers, dentists, *etc.*

London doctors and dental surgeons, 1923-24. Grafton Publishing, 1923. Directory.

See also Barbers (for Barber Surgeons)

Guys Hospital
WILKS, SAMUEL, & BETTANY, G.T. *A biographical history of Guy's Hospital.* Ward, Lock, Bowden & Co., 1892.

Kings College
LYLE, HERBERT WILLOUGHBY. *Kings and some King's men: being a record of the Medical Department of Kings College, London, from 1830 to 1909, and of Kings College Medical School from 1909 to 1934.* Oxford University Press, 1935. Includes various extensive lists of medical men. For addenda, see:

LYLE, H.W. *An addendum to 'Kings and some Kings men (London)', being an added record of Kings College Hospital and of Kings College Hospital Medical School to 5 July 1948.* Oxford University Press, 1950.

Middlesex Hospital
SAUNDERS, HILARY ST.GEORGE. *The Middlesex Hospital, 1745-1948.* Max Parris, 1949. Includes lists of various officers.

Royal College of Physicians
CLARK, GEORGE, SIR. *A history of the Royal College of Physicians of London.* 3 vols. Oxford: Clarendon Press, 1964-72. General history. Vol.3 is by A.M. Cooke.

HORWOOD, ALFRED J. 'The manuscripts of the College of Physicians, Pall Mall East, London', in HISTORICAL MANUSCRIPTS COMMISSION *Eighth report ... Report and appendix (part 1).* H.M.S.O., 1881, 226-35.

MUNK, WILLIAM. *The roll of the Royal College of Physicians of London, comprising biographical sketches of all the eminent physicians whose names are recorded in the annals from ... 1518 to ... 1825.* 2nd ed. 3 vols. Harrison and Sons, 1878. This is continued by:
BROWN, G.H. *Lives of the fellows of the Royal College of Physicians of London, 1826-1925.* The College, 1955. Sometimes referred to as Munk's *Roll ...* vol. 4. Further supplements have been edited by Richard R. Trail, to 1965, and Gordon Wolstenholme, to 1975 and 1983.

Royal College of Surgeons
BECK, R. THEODORE. *The cutting edge: early history of the Surgeons of London.* Lund Humphries, 1974. Includes biographical notes, some wills, *etc.*
COPE, ZACHARY. *The Royal College of Surgeons of England: a history.* Anthony Blond, 1959. Includes short biographies of leading surgeons, plus lists of presidents and members of council from 1800.
LE FANU, R. 'The archives of the College and its predecessor, the Company of Surgeons', *Annals of the Royal College of Surgeons of England* **12**(4), 1953, 282-5. Brief description.
PLARR, VICTOR GUSTAVE. *Plarr's lives of the fellows of The Royal College of Surgeons of England,* revised by Sir D'Arcy Power, Walter George Spencer, & Edward Gask. 2 vols. Bristol: J. Wright & Sons, for the Royal College of Surgeons, 1930. Continued by:
POWER, D'ARCY, SIR. *Lives of the fellows of the Royal College of Surgeons of England, 1930-1951.* The College, 1953.
ROYAL COLLEGE OF SURGEONS. *List of the members, fellows and licentiates in midwifery of the Royal College of Surgeons.* The College, 1825-64. Continued by: ROYAL COLLEGE OF SURGEONS *List of the fellows and members ...* The College, 1865-1965.
WALL, CECIL. *The history of the Surgeons Company, 1745-1800.* Hutchinsons, 1937. Includes lists of officers, *etc.*

Royal Medical and Chirurgical Society
MOORE, NORMAN, & PAGET, STEPHEN. *The Royal Medical and Chirurgical Society of London. Centenary, 1805-1905.* [Aberdeen]: Aberdeen University Press, 1905. Includes brief biographies of presidents.

St.Bartholomews Hospital
LAWRENCE, SUSAN C. 'Desirous of improvements in medicine: pupils and practitioners in the medical societies at Guy's and St.Bartholomew's Hospitals, 1795-1815', *Bulletin of the history of medicine* **59**, 1985, 89-104. General discussion, citing various sources and other works.
MEDVEI, VICTOR CORNELIUS, & THORNTON, JOHN, eds. *The Royal Hospital of St. Bartholemew, 1123-1973.* The Hospital, 1974. Includes KERLING, NELLIE J.M. 'Chronological list of physicians and surgeons', THORNTON, JOHN L. 'Chronological list of heads of departments in the medical college', KERLING, NELLIE J.M. 'Archives', and a wide variety of historical essays.
These are the names of the students of St. Bartholemew's Hospital who lost their lives in the Great War 1914 to 1918. Chiswick Press, 1926. Includes brief biographies.

Members of Parliament
Middlesex Members of Parliament are listed in: 'List of Middlesex knights of the shire from 1295-1832', *T.L.M.A.S.* N.S. **6**, 1933, 343-57.
See also:
ARNOLD, JACQUES A., ed. *A history of Britain's Parliamentary constituencies: the constituencies of Greater London.* 2nd ed. 3 vols. West Malling: Patricia Arnold, 1993. Lists all candidates, with votes received since 1885.
SMITH, COLIN. 'The parliamentary representation of Hornsey', *Hornsey Historical Society Bulletin* **26**, 1985, 4-9. Brief biographies of M.P.'s, 1885-1983.
CARTER, PETER. *Islington at Westminster: the story of members of Parliament for Islington and Finsbury 1884-1983.* Islington Fabian Society, 1984. Includes appendix giving biographical details.

Mercers

DOOLITTLE, IAN. *The Mercers Company 1519-1959,* ed. Peter Nailor. Mercers Hall, 1991. General history.

IMRAY, JEAN M. 'Les bones gentes de la Mercerye de Londres: a study of the membership of the medieval Mercers Company', in HOLLAENDER, A.E.J., & KELLAWAY, WILLIAM., eds. *Studies in London history presented to Philip Edmund Jones.* Hodder, 1969, 155-78. Study of the warden's account book, 14-15th c.

LYELL, LAETITIA, & WATNEY, FRANK D. *Acts of Court of the Mercer's Company, 1453-1527.* Cambridge: C.U.P., 1936. Gives many names.

NICHOLS, JOHN GOUGH. 'Remarks on the mercers and other trading companies of London, followed by some account of the records of the Mercers Company', *T.L.M.A.S.* 4(1), 1871, 131-47.

Merchant Adventurers

IMRAY, JEAN M. 'The Merchant Adventurers and their records', in RANGER, FELICITY., ed. *Prisca munimenta: studies in archival and administrative history.* University of London Press, 1973, 229-39.

Merchant Taylors

CLODE, CHARLES M. *The early history of the Guild of Merchant Taylors of the Fraternity of St.John the Baptist, London, with notices of the lives of some of its eminent members.* 2 vols. Harrison and Sons, 1888.

CLODE, CHARLES MATHEW. *Memorials of the Guild of Merchant Taylors of the fraternity of St.John the Baptist in the City of London and of its associated charities and institutions.* Harrison and Sons, 1875. Includes extensive extracts from records, biographical notes on various honorary members, and scholars of the School, *etc.*

COKAYNE, G.E. 'Merchant Taylor's Company', *M.G.H.* 2nd series **5,** 1894, 289-90, 318-9, 330-31, 339-40, 364-5 & 371-3. Record of apprentices, freedoms, *etc.,* 1562-1618.

COKAYNE, G.E. 'Freemen of Merchant Taylors', *M.G.H.* 3rd series **1,** 19-21. 16-18th c.

HOPKINSON, HENRY LENNOX, SIR. *Report on the ancient records in the possession of the Guild of Merchant Taylors of the Fraternity of St John Baptist in the City of London.* Waterlow and Sons, 1915. Includes 'list of masters and wardens from 1300 to 1561'.

SAYLE, R.T.D. *A brief history of the Worshipful Company of Merchant Taylors of the fraternity of St.John Baptist in the City of London.* Eastern Press, 1945.

SAYLE, R.T.D. *Lord Mayors' pageants of the Merchant Taylors' Company in the 15th, 16th & 17th centuries.* Privately printed, 1931. Includes brief biographies of 22 lord mayors belonging to the company, 15-17th c.

Merchants

There are many works dealing with London's merchants. The following select list is arranged in rough chronological order.

COBB, H.S., ed. *The overseas trade of London: Exchequer customs accounts, 1480-1.* L.R.S. **27.** 1990. Many names of merchants.

WILLAN, T.S. *The Muscovy merchants of 1555.* Manchester: Manchester University Press, 1953. Includes biographical dictionary.

DIETZ, BRIAN, ed. *The port and trade of early Elizabethan London: documents.* L.R.S. **8.** 1972. Primarily an edition of a port book, 1567/8, recording the names of many merchants.

LANG, ROBERT G. 'London's Aldermen in business, 1600-1625', *Gl.M.* **3**(4), 1971, 242-64. Includes list of 73 subscribers to a voyage of 1599.

LANG, R.G. 'Social origins and social aspirations of Jacobean London merchants', *Economic history review* **27,** 1974, 28-47. General discussion.

CROFT, PAULINE. *The Spanish Company.* L.R.S. **9.** 1973. Includes an edition of the Company's register book, 1604-6, giving many names of merchants.

BALDERSTON. M., ed. *James Claypoole's letter book, London and Philadelphia, 1681-1684.* San Marino: Huntington Library, 1967. Many names of merchants, *etc;* also list of ships' masters taken from the London port books.

SUTHERLAND, LUCY S. *A London merchant 1695-1774.* Oxford University Press, 1933. Study of William Braund; includes list of merchants trading with Portugal, list of insurance brokers who underwrote for William Braund, and list of ships under the management of Samuel Braund, with names and occupations of owners.

TAYLOR, G.A., ed. 'A list of London merchants and traders trading with New England A.D. 1710', *Genealogists' magazine* 8(2), 1938, 86. From the Massachusetts state archives.

MASON, FRANCES NORTON, ed. *John Norton & Sons, merchants of London and Virginia: being the papers from their counting house for the years 1750 to 1795.* Newton Abbot: David & Charles, 1968. Includes biographical appendix.

KELLOCK, KATHARINE A. 'London merchants and the pre-1776 American debts', *G.S.L.H.* 1, 1973-5, 109-49. List, with biographical notes, of London creditors claiming losses in the American War of Independence.

Mid-Wives

See Medical Professions

Millers

BUTLER, ANTHONY D. *Upminster Mill.* Davis, 1968. Includes useful information on the Nokes and Abraham families, 19-20th c.

FARRIES, K.G., & MASON, T. *The windmills of Surrey and Inner London.* Charles Skilton, 1966. Gives names of millers, *etc.*

Mineral Water Manufacturers

SANDOW, MIKE. 'H.J. Glover: high class lemonade: celebrated ginger beer', *East London record* 6, 1983, 13-16. Includes list of mineral water manufacturers, 1885-1910.

Minstrels

INGRAM, WILLIAM. 'Minstrels in Elizabethan London: who were they, what did they do?', *English literary renaissance* 14, 1984, 29-54. Includes list with biographical notes.

Missionaries

MORISON, JOHN. *The fathers and founders of the London Missionary Society.* 2 vols. Fisher, Son & Co., 1840. Brief biographies of missionaries.

Moneyers

CHALLIS, C.E., ed. *A new history of the Royal Mint.* Cambridge: C.U.P., 1992. Includes list of 'mint contracts, 1279-1817', giving many names of moneyers.

CHALLIS, C.E. 'Mint officials and moneyers of the Stuart period', *British numismatic journal* 59, 1989, 157-97. List.

CRAIG, JOHN, SIR. *The Mint: a history from A.D. 287 to 1948.* Cambridge: Cambridge University Press, 1953. Includes index of persons with their Mint connexions.

NIGHTINGALE, PAMELA. 'Some London moneyers, and reflections on the organisation of English mints in the 11th and 12th centuries', *Numismatic chronicle* 142, 1982, 34-50.

Musicians

BAILLIE, HUGH. 'Some biographical notes on English church musicians, chiefly working in London (1485-1569)', *R[oyal] M[usical] A[ssociation] research chronicle* 2, 1962, 18-57. Biographical dictionary.

ARKWRIGHT, G.E.P. 'Notes on the parish registers of St. Helen's, Bishopsgate, London', *Musical antiquary* 1, 1909, 41-4. Extracts relating to musicians.

FISKE, ROGER. *English theatre music in the 18th century.* Oxford University Press, 1973. Includes biographies of singers, index of composers, and many names of musicians.

H., A.F. 'Musicians named in the registers of St. James's, Garlickhithe', *Musical antiquary* 3, 1911-12, 237-8. Brief extracts.

'An 18th century directory of London musicians', *Galpin Society journal* 2, 1949, 27-31. Reprinted from Mortimers *London Universal directory,* 1763. Alphabetical lists of 'masters and professors of music' and 'musical instrument-makers, including organ-builders'.

Philharmonic Society

FOSTER, MYLES BIRKET. *History of the Philharmonic Society of London, 1813-1912: a record of a hundred years' work in the cause of music.* John Lane, 1912. Many musicians mentioned.

Royal College of Music

COLLES, H.C., & CRUFT, JOHN. *The Royal College of Music: a centenary record 1883-1983.* Prince Consort Foundation, 1982. Includes list of fellows.

Royal Society of Musicians

MATTHEWS, BETTY. *The Royal Society of Musicians of Great Britain: list of members, 1738-1984.* The Society, 1985. With brief biographical notes.

Worshipful Company of Musicians

CREWDSON, H.A.M. *A short history of the Worshipful Company of Musicians.* Constable, 1950. Includes list of masters from 1780, and clerks from 1700.

Handbook of the Worshipful Company of Musicians. 3rd ed. The Company, 1915. Includes roll of contemporary members, with addresses, dates of admission, *etc.*

See also Actors, Choristers, Minstrels, Organists and Playing Card Makers.

Needlemakers

[PRICE, J.E.] *The Worshipful Company of Needlemakers of the City of London, with a list of the court of assistants and livery.* Robson and Sons, 1876.

WEBB, CLIFF. *London livery companies apprenticeship registers, Volume 9. Needlemakers Company, 1664-1801; Pinmakers Company, 1691-1723.* Society of Genealogists, 1997.

Nurse Children

CLARK, GILLIAN. 'London's first evacuees: a population study of nurse children', *Local historian* **19**, 1989, 100-106. Discussion of children sent out of the capital for nursing, based on parish registers.

CLARK, GILLIAN. 'A study of nurse children 1550-1750', *Local population studies* **39**, 1987, 8-23.

Nursemaids

CLARK, GILLIAN. 'London nurse children: a source of female employment in the rural domestic economy between 1540 and 1750', *Genealogists' magazine* **23**, 1989, 97-101. General discussion of sources for women who fostered children in the Home Counties.

Nurserymen

DURBAN, IAN. '... noted for extensive market-ground ... : the market gardeners of West Middlesex', *W.M.* **7**(3), 1988, 114-5. Includes names from Pigot's *Directory,* 1840.

HARVEY, JOHN H. 'Mid-Georgian nurseries of the London region', *T.L.M.A.S.* **26**, 1975, 293-308. Gazetteer, naming nurserymen.

HARVEY, JOHN H. 'The nurseries on Milne's land-use map', *T.L.M.A.S.* **24**, 1973, 177-98. Gazetteer of nurseries c.1795-9, giving names of nurserymen.

See also Gardeners

Chelsea, etc.

WILLSON, ELEANOR JOAN. *West London nursery gardens: the nursery gardens: the nursery gardens of Chelsea, Fulham, Hammersmith, Kensington and a part of Westminster, founded before 1900.* Fulham & Hammersmith Historical Society, 1982. Many names.

Chiswick

WILLSON, E.J. 'Some Chiswick nurseries', *Brentford & Chiswick Local History Society journal* **4**, 1985, 4-6. Especially relating to the Dancer and Fromow families.

Edmonton

BURNBY, J.G.L., & ROBINSON, A.E. *Now turned into fair garden plots (Stow).* Occasional paper N.S. **45**. E.H.H.S., 1983. Includes catalogue of commercial horticulturalists.

Feltham

BEAMSON, MARY. 'The nursery and market gardeners of Feltham', *Honeslaw chronicle* **9**(1), 1986, 3-6. 18-19th c.

Hackney

SOLMAN, DAVID. 'The lost botanical nurseries of Hackney', *The Terrier: the Friends of Hackney Archives newsletter* **24**, 1991, 2-4. Includes notes on nurserymen.

Twickenham

URWIN, A.C.B. *Commercial nurseries and market gardens.* B.T.L.H.S. paper **50**, 1982. Includes list of nurserymen, 19th c.

Nurses

HOWLETT, BRIDGET. 'Records of nurses and nursing: resources in London Metropolitan Archives', *Genealogists' magazine* **26**(6), 1999, 213-7.

Opera Singers

ROLLINS, CYRIL, & WITTS, RAWDON JOHN. *The D'Oyly Carte Opera Company in Gilbert and Sullivan operas: a record of productions 1875-1961.* Michael Joseph, 1962. Includes names of performers and staff *etc.*

Opticians

See Spectacle Makers

Organists

DAWE, DONOVAN. *Organists of the City of London: a record of one thousand organists with an annotated index.* The author, 1983.

PEARCE, CHARLES WILLIAM. *Notes on old London city churches: their organs, organists and musical associations.* Vincent Music Co., 1908. Includes notes on organists.

All Souls, Langham Place

GOULDEN, COLIN. *The organs and organists of All Souls, Langham Place.* The Church, 1988. Since 1824.

Chapel Royal

SHAW, WATKINS. *The succession of organists of the Chapel Royal and the Cathedrals of England and Wales from c.1538; also of the organists of the Collegiate churches of Westminster and Windsor, certain academic choral foundations, and the cathedrals of Armagh and Dublin.* Oxford: Clarendon Press, 1991. Detailed biographical notes.

Saint Katherine Cree

CAMPBELL, K.E. 'Organists of St. Katherine Cree church', *Organ* **67**, 1988, 121-5. Biographical notes, 16-20th c.

St.Margarets, Westminster

SUMNER, W.L. 'The organs and organists of St.Margaret's, Westminster', *Organ* **45**(179), 1966, 106-12. Includes list of organists, 1616-1929.

St.Pauls Cathedral

BUMPUS, JOHN S. *The organists & composers of S.Pauls Cathedral.* Bowden Hudson & Co., 1891. Includes a biographical dictionary.

Westminster Abbey

RIMBAULT, EDWARD FRANCIS. 'The organs and organists of Westminster Abbey', *Notes and queries* 3rd series **10**, 1866, 181-4. Includes brief biographical notes, 16-19th c.

Painters

COX-JOHNSON, ANN. *Handlist of painters, sculptors and architects associated with St.Marylebone, 1760-1960.* Borough of St.Marylebone Public Libraries Committee, 1963.

ENGLEFIELD, W.A.D. *History of the Painter-Stainers Company of London.* Chapman and Dodd, 1923. General; includes lists of officers, 14-20th c.

ENGLEFIELD, W.A.D. *The history of the Painter-Stainers Company of London.* 2nd issue. Hazell Watson & Viney, 1950. Includes list of officers from 1578. Continued by:

ARNOLD, A.P., & INGRAM, A.G. *The history of the Painters-Stainers Company of London, volume II.* [The Company], 1988.

SURRY, NIGEL. 'Hampshire apprentices to the Painter Stainers Company: their professional activities and social origins, c. 1660-1795', *Proceedings of the Hampshire Field Club and Archaeological Society* **37**, 1981, 63-71. Includes list of masters and apprentices, 1660-1795.

See also Lawyers. Lincolns Inn

41

Parish Clerks

ADAMS, REGINALD. *The parish clerks of London: a history of the Worshipful Company of Parish Clerks of London.* Phillimore, 1971. Includes list of masters, 1448-1970, calendar of the Company's archives, *etc.*

CHRISTIE, JAMES. *Parish clerks: some account of parish clerks, more especially of the ancient fraternity (bretherne and sisterne) of S.Nicholas, now known as the Worshipful Company of Parish Clerks.* Privately printed, 1893. Includes analysis of the bede roll, 1448-1521, giving names of masters.

EBBLEWHITE, ERNEST ARTHUR. *The Parish Clerks' Company and its charters; with a biographical calendar and an inventory of its property between 1610 and 1705.* Privately printed, 1932.

Pattenmakers

FITCH, CHARLES. *The history of the Worshipful Company of Pattenmakers of the City of London.* Bungay: Richard Clay & Sons, 1926. General account, with some extracts from original sources.

WEBB CLIFF. *London livery company apprenticeship registers, volume 13. Pattenmakers Company, 1673-1805.* Society of Genealogists, 1998.

Paviors

FALDO, WALTER A. K., ed. *History of the Worshipful Company of Paviors of the City of London.* 3rd ed. The Company, 1966. Includes list of masters, 1889-1966, and many names.

WEBB, CLIFF. *London livery companies apprenticeship registers, Volume 20. Paviors' Company, 1568-1800.* Society of Genealogists, 1998.

WELCH, CHARLES. *History of the Worshipful Company of Paviors of the City of London.* 2nd ed. The Company, 1932. Includes list of members in 1932.

Pawnbrokers

PRICE, F.G. HILTON. 'Some notes upon the signs of the pawnbrokers in London in the seventeenth and eighteenth centuries', *Archaeological journal* **59**, 1902, 160-200. Includes list of pawnbrokers.

Pepperers

MATTHEWS, LESLIE G. *The pepperers, spicers and apothecaries of London during the thirteenth and fourteenth centuries.* Society of Apothecaries of London Faculty of the History and Philosophy of Medicine and Pharmacy, 1980. Biographical dictionary of 260 tradesmen.

Pewterers

COTTERELL, HOWARD H., & HEAL, AMBROSE. 'Pewterers trade cards', *The Connoisseur* **76**, 1926, 221-6. Brief note.

COTTERELL, HOWARD HERSCHEL. 'Pewterers trade cards of the seventeenth century', *The Connoisseur* **78**, 1927, 25-7.

COTTERELL, HOWARD H., & HEAL, AMBROSE, SIR. 'About pewterers trade cards', *The Connoisseur* **80**, 1928, 81-90.

HOWARD, RONALD F. 'Medieval London pewterers', *Pewter Society journal* **4**, 1983, 47-53. Brief study; includes pedigree of Syward, 14th c.

HOMER, RONALD F. 'The medieval pewterers of London, c.1190-1457', *T.L.M.A.S.* **36**, 1985, 137-63. Includes list.

HOOPER, P.R. 'Early 19th c. London pewterers', *Journal of the Pewter Society* 4(3), 1984, 81-3. Brief notes from the trade directories.

HOMER, RONALD F. 'Medieval London pewterers', *Pewter Society journal* **4**, 1983, 47-53. Brief study; includes pedigree of Syward, 14th c.

MARKHAM, C.A. *The new pewter marks and old pewter ware, domestic and ecclesiastical ...* 2nd ed. Reeves and Turner, 1928. Includes 'index of members of the Pewterers' Company, and of pewter workers'; also 'list of freemen of the Company of Pewterers'.

WELCH, CHARLES. *History of the Worshipful Company of Pewterers of the City of London, based upon their own records.* 2 vols. Blades, East & Blades, 1902. Mainly abstracts of original sources, with many names.

'London pewterers in 1669', *Reliquary* N.S. **6**, 1892, 50-51. Lists prominent members of the trade.

42

Philanthropists

ANDREW, DONNA T. *Philanthropy and police: London charity in the eighteenth century.* Princeton: Princeton University Press, 1989. Includes extensive list of philanthropists.

Photographers

PRITCHARD, MICHAEL. *A directory of London photographers, 1841-1908.* Rev. ed. Watford: Photoresearch, 1994. Lists over 2,500 photographers, with addresses and dates.

Physicians

See Medics

Piano Makers

HARDING, ROSAMOND, E.M. *The piano-forte: its history traced to the Great Exhibition of 1851.* 2nd ed. Gresham Books, 1978. Includes 'select list of English pianoforte makers in London and its environs up to the year 1851.'

Picture Dealers

AGNEW, GEOFFREY. *Agnew's, 1817-1967.* Bradbury Agnew Press, 1967. Picture dealers; includes pedigree of Agnew, 18-20th c., also lists of staff.

Pinmakers

See Needlemakers

Pipemakers

ATKINSON, DAVID, & OSWALD, ADRIAN. 'London clay tobacco pipes', *Journal of the British Archaeological Association* 3rd series **32**, 1969, 171-227. Includes list of makers, 17-19th c.

ATKINSON, D.R. '19th century marked pipes from Maverton Road, Bow, East London', *T.L.M.A.S.* **28**, 1977, 258-68. Gives some names of pipemakers.

OSWALD, ADRIAN. 'New light on some 18th-century pipemakers of London', in BIRD, JOANNA, CHAPMAN, HUGH, & CLARK, JOHN., eds. *Collectanea Londiniensia: studies in London history and archaeology presented to Ralph Merrifield.* Special paper **2**. London and Middlesex Archaeological Society, 1978, 346-75. Includes list.

WALKER, IAIN C. 'Some notes on the Westminster and London Tobacco-Pipe Makers' Guild', *T.L.M.A.S.* **23**(1), 1971, 78-89. Includes lists of officers, 1663 and 1821. *See also* Playing Card Makers

Plateworkers

See Goldsmiths

Players

See Actors

Playing Card Makers

WEBB, CLIFF. *London livery company apprenticeship registers, Volume 12. Makers of Playing Cards' Company, 1675-1760; Musicians Company, 1765-1800; Saddlers Company 1657-1666, 1800; Tobaccopipemakers Company 1800.* Society of Genealogists, 1998.

Plumbers

WALDO, F.J. *A short history of the Worshipful Company of Plumbers of the City of London.* 2nd ed. The Company, 1923. Includes a list of records, and of liverymen in 1923, *etc.*

WEBB, CLIFF. *London livery company apprenticeship registers, vol.33. Plumbers Company, 1571-1800.* Society of Genealogists, 2000. Not seen.

Policemen

BAZZONE, ALAN. 'Another police force of East London', *C.A.* **43**, 1989, 3-4. Brief note on records of Dock Company Forces.

BROWN, BERNARD. 'Metropolitan police history & ancestry', *C.A.* **57**, 1993, 41-2. Brief note.

BROWN, BERNARD. 'The Middlesex constabulary', *Journal of the Police History Society* **8**, 1993, 64-8. Discusses the organisational history of Middlesex police.

FORESTER, CHRIS. 'Metropolitan Police consolidated index', *Journal of the Police History Society* **9**, 1994, 41-2.

FORESTER, CHRIS. 'Indexers and their indexes: the Metropolitan Police consolidated index', *Family tree magazine* **10**(9), 1994, 41.

FOUNTAIN, MICHAEL. 'My ancestor was a policeman', *Metropolitan* **18**(3), 1996, 135-6. Tracing ancestors in the Metropolitan Police.

HARDWICKE, GLYN. *Keepers of the door: the history of the Port of London Authority police.* Port Press for the Port of London Authority Police, 1980. Includes lists of police killed on duty, and of those who won decorations or awards.

HOWGRAVE-GRAHAM, H.M. *The Metropolitan Police at war.* H.M.S.O., 1947. Lists 700 officers killed, 1939-45; also honours and awards.

JONES, D. 'Was your ancestor a police constable', *Greentrees* **10**(3), 1991, 54-55. List from the 1841-81 censuses for Wembley.

PORTER, BERNARD JOHN. *The origins of the vigilant state: the London Metropolitan Police Special Branch before the First World War.* Weidenfeld and Nicolson, 1987. General study with some names.

SHORROCKS, JOHN. 'Parish constable to police constable, and Metropolitan police records', *North West Kent family history* **3**(7), 1984, 223-6. Discussion of sources.

REAY, W.T. *The Specials: how they served London: the story of the Metropolitan Special Constabulary.* William Heinemann, 1920. Includes many photographic portraits of senior officers during the First World War.

SHPAYER-MAKOV, HAIA. 'The appeal of country workers: the case of the Metropolitan Police', *Historical research* **64**, 1991, 186-203. Recruitment from the shires.

Metropolitan Police Offices: Office of the Commissioner: correspondence and papers (MEPO2): class list. List and Index Society **138** & **146**, 1977-8.

The Peeler: the Friends of the Metropolitan Police Museum magazine. 1996- .

See also Bow Street Runners

Porters

STERN, WALTER M. *The porters of London.* Longmans, Green & Co., 1960. General study, some names.

See also Shipbrokers / Owners.

Postmen

BAGUST, F. *Some notes on the small post offices of London in the seventeenth and eighteenth centuries.* Bournemouth: Bournemouth Guardian, 1937. Includes names and addresses of 'letter receivers'.

JAY, BARRIE. *The British county catalogue of postal history, Volume 3, London,* ed. R.M. Willcocks & B. Jay. R.M. Willcocks, 1983. Includes incomplete list of 'London general post receivers.'

PHILLIPS, ADRIAN. 'Post Office Headquarters Record Office', *C.A.* **14**, 1982, 13-16. Includes list of recruits in London, 1824-39.

'The Post Offices of Pinner', *The Pinn* **2**, 1986, 9-10. Gives biographical notes on postmasters.

Potters

BRITTON, FRANK. *London delftware.* Jonathan Horn, 1987. Includes list of 450 18th c. potters — mainly in Wapping, Southwark, Lambeth, Putney and Isleworth.

EDWARDS, RHODA. *London potters circa 1570-1714.* Journal of ceramic history **6**. Stafford: George Street Press, 1974. List with biographical notes.

Poulters

JONES, P.E. *The Worshipful Company of Poulters of the City of London: a short history.* 2nd ed. Oxford University Press, 1965. Includes list of masters, 1618-1964, with some biographical notes.

WEBB, CLIFF. *London livery company apprenticeship registers, Volume 18. Poulters Company, 1691-1729, 1754-1800.* Society of Genealogists, 1998.

Printers
See Book Trades

Publishers
See Book Trades

Pupils
See School Pupils and Teachers

Railway Contractors & Engineers

POPPLEWELL, LAWRENCE. *A gazetteer of the railway contractors and engineers of South East England, 1830-1914.* Ferndown: Melledgen Press, 1983.

Rat Catchers
CUFLEY, DAVID. 'The rat-catchers of Enfield', *N.M.* 7(2), 1984/5, 41-3.

Recorders
See Local Government Officers

Rowers
PAGE, GEOFFREY. *Hear the boat sing: the history of Thames Rowing Club and tideway rowing.* Kingswood Press, 1991. Includes lists of crews, *etc.*
WELLS, HENRY BRIANT. *Vesta Rowing Club: a centenary history.* The Club, 1969. Includes two lists of winners of events, and list of principal officers.

Saddlers
SHERWELL, JOHN W. *History of the Guild of Saddlers of the City of London.* 3rd ed. rev. Kenneth S. Laurie. Chelmsford: J.H. Clarke & Co., 1956. Includes list of masters, roll of honour, *etc.*
See also Playing Card Makers

Salters
WATSON, J. STEVEN. *A history of the Salters Company.* Oxford University Press, 1963. Includes list of masters from 1611.

School Pupils and Teachers, *etc.*
The records of schools, colleges, and other educational establishments provide much information on pupils, teachers, school governors, benefactors, and others connected with education. For the metropolis, much information from these records has been published. The list which follows is not intended to be a comprehensive listing of everything published on the history of education in London; rather, its aim is to identify works which have particular value to the genealogist. School registers are particularly valuable; also useful are the many school histories which identify former teachers and students.
For a detailed and important listing of the records of over 2,000 London schools, see:
WEBB, CLIFF. *An Index of London schools and their records.* Society of Genealogists, 1999. Covers the area of the old London County Council.

A number of other general works may also be cited:
WIDE, S.M., & MORRIS, J.A. 'The episcopal licensing of schoolmasters in the Diocese of London 1627-1685', *Gl.M.* 2(9), 1967, 392-406. Study of the subscription books; the authors' index to them is in the Greater London Record Office.
'Education in London before 1870: a handlist of selected items in Guildhall Library', *Gl.M.* 3(3), 1970, 218-32. Lists many school histories; lists of pupils, etc., including manuscript material.
A list of patrons of the anniversary of the Charity-Schools MDCCCXLII. Norris and Son, 1842. Extensive listing, with addresses. The charity schools concerned are those of London, Westminster, Southwark and environs.

A. *Schools*

Acton
HARPER SMITH, A., & T. *Acton schools 1817-1965.* Acton past and present **13**. Acton History Group, 1987. Lists various schools.

Adult Orphan Institution
CLARKE, DONALD. *A daisy in the broom: the story of a school, 1820-1958.* Broughton: Julia London, 1991. History of the Adult Orphan Institution; includes some names.

Charterhouse
The school moved from Charterhouse to Godalming in Surrey in 1872.
QUICK, ANTHONY. *Charterhouse: a history of the school.* James & James, 1990. Includes a 'selected list of Old Carthusians'.
SMITH-DAMPIER, J.L. *Carthusian worthies.* Oxford: Basil Blackwell, 1940. Many brief biographies.
CHANCELLOR, FRANCIS BERESFORD, & ELLIS, HENRY S. *Celebrated Carthusians.* Philip Allen, 1936. Biographies of 25 old boys.
MARSH, BOWER, & CRISP, FREDERICK ARTHUR, eds. *Alumni Carthusiani: a record of the foundation scholars of Charterhouse, 1614-1872.* Grove Park Press, 1913. Includes biographical notes; also lists staff, governors and incumbents of Charterhouse livings.

School Pupils and Teachers *cont.*

ARROWSMITH, R.L., ed. *Charterhouse register, 1769-1872, with appendix of non-foundationers, 1614-1769.* Phillimore, 1974.

PARISH, W.D. *List of Carthusians 1800 to 1879.* Lewes: Farncombe & Co., 1879. Charterhouse School register.

JAMESON, E.M., et al. *Charterhouse register 1872-1931.* 3rd ed. 2 vols. Guildford: Old Carthusian Club, 1932.

Christs Hospital

PEARCE, E.H. *Annals of Christs Hospital.* 2nd ed. Hugh Rees, 1908. General history; includes lists of presidents, treasurers, heads, and clerks.

ROBERTS, H.A. *The records of the Amicable Society of Blues and its predecessors from 1629 to 1895.* Cambridge: Cambridge University Press, 1924. This was the old boys society of Christ's Hospital. Includes list of members in 1923, *etc.*

TROLLOPE, WILLIAM. *A history of the royal foundation of Christ's Hospital, with an account of the plan of education, the internal economy of the Institution, and memoirs of eminent blues, preceded by a narrative of the rise, progress, and suppression of the Convent of the Grey Friars of London.* William Pickering, 1834. School history.

ALLAN, GEORGE A.T. *Christs Hospital exhibitors to the Universities of Oxford and Cambridge, 1566-1923.* Harrison & Sons, 1924.

ALLAN, G.A.T. 'Records of Christs Hospital', *Genealogists' magazine* 7, 1935-7, 161-71. *Christ's Hospital admissions.* Harrison and Sons, 1937. Vol.1. 1554-99. No more published.

City of London School

DOUGLAS-SMITH, A.E. *The City of London School.* 2nd ed. Oxford: Basil Blackwell, 1965. Includes an extensive biographical index of persons mentioned in the text.

Clergy Orphan School

SIMMONDS, MARK JOHN. *Register of the Clergy Orphan School for Boys, 1751-1896.* Canterbury: St.Augustines College, 1897. The school had various moves; it was in Yorkshire, 1751-1804, Acton, 1804-12, St.Johns Wood, 1812-55, and Canterbury, 1855-96. It took boys from all over the country.

Collingwood

SCOTT, CHRISTIAN KEITH. *With the colours: Collingwood and Heckford Street old scholars.* Ratcliff Settlement, 1917. List, noting company and some home addresses.

Dugard's School

HART, G. 'The register of a private school for boys at St.Peter's Hill, London, 1650', *Genealogists magazine* 3(1), 1927, 27-30.

HART, G. 'The register of a private school for boys at St.Peter's Hill, London, 1650', *N.M.* 4(2), 1981/2, 109-12. Register of Thomas Dugard's private school; many names.

Edmonton

See Latymer School

Elisha Biscoe School

ERRINGTON, A.J. 'The Elisha Biscoe School', *Transactions of the Southall Historical Society* 1, 1960, 11-28. 18-20th c., includes notes on the Biscoe family, and extracts from the will of Elisha Biscoe, 1776, and the family's arms.

Emanuel School

SCOTT-GILES, C. WILFRED, & SLATER, BERNARD V. *The history of Emanuel School, 1594-1964.* The Old Emanuel Association, 1966. Includes a chapter on the medieval Dacre family.

French Protestant School

BEAUFORT, W.M. *Records of the French Protestant School, founded by Huguenot refugees, 1747.* Lymington: Chas. T. King, 1894. Alphabetical listing of pupils, with brief notes.

MINET, SUSAN. 'Ecole de Charité Francaise de Westminster', *Pr.Hug.Soc.L.* 13, 1923-9, 374-92. Includes list of girls, 1871-1923.

MINET, SUSAN. 'Ecole de Charité Francaise de Westminster', *Pr.Hug.Soc.L.* 12, 1917-23, 91-117. Includes list of officers and directors 1752-1900; also supplements: 'Records of the French Protestant School founded by Huguenot refugees, 1747', *Pr.Hug.Soc.L.* 4, 1891-3, 355-466. Register, 18-19th c.

'The Westminster French Protestant School', *Pr.Hug.Soc.L.* 2, 1887-88, 464-8. Includes list of benefactors, 1750-1883.

Greycoat Hospital
DAY, E.S. *An old Westminster endowment, being a history of the Grey Coat Hospital as recorded in the minute books.* Rees, 1902. School history.

Grosvenor School
RIDGE, MARGARET. 'Grosvenor School, Holly Road', *W.M.* 7(2), 1988, 68-9. 1881 census for a Twickenham school.

Hackney Downs School
'Hackney Downs School, formerly the Grocers' Company's School, 1876-1926', *C.A.* 49, 1990-91, 11-14. Includes many names, with roll of honour 1914-18.

Hammersmith
WORRALL, EDW. S. 'A list of Hammersmith Convent School pensioners', *L.R.* 2, 1972, 15-18. 'Pensioners' means pupils; 1677-83. 'Richard Elwell of Hammersmith', *Genealogists' magazine* 14, 1962-4, 214-21. Schoolmaster; includes list of 206 pupils at his school, 1805-35.

Hampton
GARSIDE, BERNARD. *The free school of Robert Hammond in Hampton-on-Thames, and other Hampton charities during the sixteenth and seventeenth centuries.* Richmond: Dimbleby's, 1958. Includes notes on various charities, and detailed list of sources.
GARSIDE, BERNARD. *The history of Hampton School from 1556 to 1700, with a brief account of the years between 1700 and the present day.* Cambridge: Cambridge University Press, 1931. Includes chapter on the Pigeon family, wills of Robert Hammond, 1556, Edmund Pigeon, 1657, and John Jones, 1692, notes on sources, *etc.*

Harrow
HOWSON, EDMUND WHYTEHEAD, & WARNER, GEORGE TOWNSEND, eds. *Harrow School.* Arnold, 1898. Extensive.
GUN, W.T.J. *The Harrow School register, 1571-1800.* Longmans, Green & Co., 1934.
DAUGLEISH, M.G., & STEPHENSON, P.K. *The Harrow School register 1800-1911.* 3rd ed. Longmans & Co., 1911. Supersedes previous edition for 1801-1900 by R.C. Welch.

STOGDON, J.H. *The Harrow School register 1845-1925: second series.* 2 vols. Longmans Green and Co., 1925. v.1. 1845-1885; v.2. 1885-1925.
MOIR, J.W., ed. *The Harrow School register 1885-1949.* 5th ed. Rivingtons, 1951.
Harrow memorials of the Great War. 6 vols. Philip Lee Warner for Harrow School, 1918-21. Biographies of the fallen, with portraits.

Harrow County School
MAY, TREVOR. *The history of the Harrow County School for Boys.* Harrow: The School, 1975. Includes list of teachers, 20th c.

Highgate School
REEVES, E.W. *Highgate School ... A roll of the school, with names of the Governors, 1565-1913, preachers at the old chapel, 1658-1832, head masters of the school, 1572-1913, and assistant masters, 1833-1913.* 2nd ed. Unwin Brothers, 1913.
HUGHES, PATRICK, & DAVIES, IAN F., eds. *Highgate School register 1833-1988.* 7th ed. Castle Cary: Castle Cary Press, 1988/9. There are various other editions of this register.

Islington
'A list of the boys new admitted (thought to be to the Islington parochial school)', *Metropolitan* 18(1), 1995, 8. For 1826.
Report from the Committee of the Parochial Schools of Islington, to the subscribers: rules and regulations, list of subscribers, &c, &c. Compton & Ritchie, 1816-33. Annual, with names and addresses of subscribers.

Islington. Bush Hill Park
'Corporal punishment at Bush Hill Park', *N.M.* 10, 1988, 37. Brief list of children punished in an Islington school, 1899 and 1900.

Jews' College
HYAMSON, ALBERT M. *Jews' College, London, 1855-1955.* Jews' College, 1955. Includes list of officers.

47

School Pupils & Teachers cont.

Jews' Free School
MOORE, EILEEN. 'The Jews' Free School', *N.M.* 4(1), 1981, 67-9. Includes list of pupils at Edmonton House, from the 1841 and 1851 censuses.

Kings College School
MILES, F.R. *Kings College School: a register of pupils in the school under the first headmaster, Dr. J.R. Major, 1831-66.* The School, 1974.

MILES, F.R. *Kings College School: a register of pupils in the school under second headmaster, Dr. G.F. Maclear and the third headmaster Dr. T.H. Stokoe.* The School, 1985. Designated 'volume 2'. Covers 1866-1889.

MILES, F.R. *Kings College School: a register of pupils in the school under the fourth headmaster, C.W. Bourne, the fifth headmaster, D.R. Smith, and the sixth headmaster, H.L. Rogers.* The School, 1988. Designated 'volume 3'. Covers 1889-1934.

Latymer School
MORRIS, JOSEPH ACTON. *A history of the Latymer School at Edmonton.* The Governors, 1975. General history, 17-20th c., includes list of long-serving teachers, 20th c.

WHEATLEY, WILLIAM. *The history of Edward Latymer and his foundation.* Rev. ed. Becclesfield: Clowes, 1953. Latymer School; includes will of Edward Latymer, 1624.

Mercers' School
'Mercers School', *T.L.M.A.S.* N.S. 1, 1905, 115-50. Includes list of masters, 1542-1879.

Merchant Taylors' School
DRAPER, FREDERICK WILLIAM MARSDEN. *Four centuries of Merchant Taylors' School, 1561-1961.* Oxford University Press, 1962. General history.

WILSON, HARRY BRISTOW. *The history of Merchant Taylors' School, from its foundation to the present time.* 2 vols. Marchant and Galabin, 1812-14. v.1. Of its founders, patrons, benefactors and masters. v.2. Of its principal scholars.

HART, E.P. *Merchant Taylors' School register, 1561-1934.* 2 vols. Merchant Taylors Company, 1936.

ROBINSON, CHARLES J. *A register of the scholars admitted into Merchant Taylors' School, from A.D. 1562 to 1874, compiled from authentic sources and edited with biographical notices.* 2 vols. Lewes: Farncombe & Co., 1882-3. Includes biographical notices of head masters.

HART, E.P. *Merchant Taylors' School register, 1851-1920.* Merchant Taylors' Company, 1923. Supersedes the edition by William Baker covering 1871-1900. Includes roll of honour, 1914-18, and lists masters.

BULLEN, R. FREEMAN. 'Suffolk boys at Merchant Taylors' School, London, 1562 to 1699', *East Anglian miscellany* **1917**, 34-5 & 36-7.

Merchant Taylor's School war list and roll of honour. Adlard & Son & West Newman, 1920.

SIMMONDS, MARK J. *Merchant Taylor fellows of St.John's College, Oxford.* Oxford University Press, 1930. Register with biographical notes, 1565-1861.

Mill Hill School
BRETT-JAMES, NORMAN G. *The history of Mill Hill School, 1807-1907.* Andrew Melrose, 1909. Includes list of masters.

HAMPDEN-COOK, ERNEST. *The register of Mill Hill School, 1807-1926.* The School, 1926.

BRETT-JAMES, NORMAN G., & GIFFORD, JOHN. *1914-1919: The book of remembrance and war record of Mill Hill School.* Reigate: T. Malcolmson, [1922?]

BRETT-JAMES, NORMAN G. *The book of remembrance and war record of Mill Hill School, 1939-1945.* Frederick Stannard at Kennerley Press, [1950?]

New Brentford
ZOUCH, CONNIE. 'The New Brentford Charity School', *W.M.* 7(4), 1989, 149-51. Many names of children, 1703-14.

North London
MOORE, EILEEN D. 'A school for girls: London, 1788', *N.M.* 2(1), 1979. List of pupils at a Masons' school in North London.

Northwood College
Northwood College record, 1878-1931. The College, [1931?]. Register of pupils.

Notting Hill & Ealing High School
SAYERS, JANE ELEANOR. *The fountain unsealed: a history of the Notting Hill and Ealing High School.* Welwyn Garden City: Broadwater Press, 1973. Many names, with some named photographs.

Owen's School
DARE, REGINALD ARTHUR. *A history of Owen's School.* Wallington: Carwal, 1963. Islington; includes list of 'Easterbrook appointments' to the staff, 19-20th c.

Roan School
KIRBY, J.W. *History of the Roan School (The Greycoat School) and its founder.* Blackheath Press, 1929. Includes list of assistant masters since 1877, of alumni in 1928, *etc.*

St.Clement Danes School
HADLEY, W. *A brief history of St.Clement Danes Grammar School.* [The School], 1951. Includes notes on eminent old boys.

St.Dunstan's College
MORRIS, L.F. *A history of St.Dunstan's College.* St.Dunstan's College, 1970. Includes various lists of staff and pupils.

St.Paul's Cathedral Choir School
St.Paul's Cathedral Choir School register. 9th ed. Congleton: Heads, 1964. From 1873.

St.Paul's School
McDONNELL, MICHAEL F.J. *A history of St.Paul's School.* Chapman and Hall, 1909. Includes much information on head masters.

McDONNELL, MICHAEL F.J. 'St.Paul's School: Old Paulines who attended its anniversary meetings in the eighteenth and early nineteenth centuries', *Notes & queries* **170**, 1936, 308-11, 328-31, 346-9, 362-6 & 380-84. Includes brief biographical notes.

MEAD, A.H. *A miraculous draught of fishes: a history of St.Paul's School.* James & James, 1990. Includes selected list of old Paulines and a select bibliography.

McDONNELL, SIR MICHAEL. *The registers of St.Paul's School, 1509-1748.* Privately printed for the Governors, 1977. Includes detailed biographical notes.

GARDINER, ROBERT BARLOW, ed. *The admission registers of St.Paul's School from 1748 to 1876.* George Bell and Sons, 1884. Includes biographical notices and notes on the earlier masters and scholars of the school from its foundation.

GARDINER, ROBERT BARLOW, ed. *The admission registers of St.Paul's School from 1876 to 1905.* Bell and Sons, 1906. With biographical notices.

MEAD, ARTHUR HUGH. ed. *St.Paul's School registers.* The School, 1990. Covers 1905-85.

St.Peter's Hill
See Dugard's School

St.Peters College
WELCH, JOSEPH. *The list of the Queen's Scholars of St.Peter's College, Westminster, admitted on that foundation since 1663, and of such as have been thence elected to Christ Church, Oxford, and Trinity College, Cambridge, from the foundation by Queen Elizabeth, 1561, to the present time ...* New ed. G.W. Ginger, 1852. Includes brief biographies.

Soho
CARDWELL, JOHN HENRY. *The story of a charity school: two centuries of popular education in Soho, 1699-1899.* Truslove, Hanson & Comba, 1899. Includes lists of masters and mistresses, prizewinners, and archives, etc.

Stationers Company School
BAYNES, ROBERT. *A history of the Stationers Company's School, 1858-1983.* The Company, 1987. Many names, including earliest list of admissions (in 1861).

Twickenham
See Grosvenor School

University College School
ORME, TEMPLE. *University College School, London: alphabetical and chronological register for 1831-1891.* H. Walton Lawrence, 1892.

49

UNIVERSITY COLLEGE SCHOOL. *Register for 1860-1931, with a short history of the school.* U.C.S. Centenary Appeal Fund, 1931.

COCKMAN, C.R., & THOMAS, C.L.R. *Roll of honour and war list, 1914-18, of University College School, Hampstead.* St.Albans: Campfield Press, [1922]. Includes brief biographical notes.

Westminster School

CARLETON, JOHN DUDLEY. *Westminster School: a history.* Rev. ed. Rupert Hart-Davis, 1965. Includes list of headmasters, etc.

FIELD, JOHN. *The King's nurseries: the story of Westminster School.* James & James, 1987. Includes brief biographical notes on prominent 'old Westminsters'.

FORSHALL, FREDERICK H. *Westminster School, past and present.* Wyman & Sons, 1884. Includes extensive index to masters and pupils.

TANNER, LAWRENCE E. *Westminster School.* 2nd ed. Country Life, 1951. General history; includes short bibliography.

WHITMORE, J.B. 'Westminster School and its records', *T.L.M.A.S.* N.S. **10**(2), 1949-50, 139-44. Brief discussion.

BARKER, G.F.R., & STENNING, ALAN H., eds. *The Westminster School register from 1764 to 1883.* Macmillan and Co., 1892.

BARKER, G.F. RUSSELL, & STENNING, ALAN. *The record of old Westminsters: biographical list of all those who are known to have been educated at Westminster School from the earliest times to 1927.* 2 vols. Chiswick Press, 1928.

WHITMORE, J.B., RADCLIFFE, G.R.Y., & SIMPSON, D.C. *The record of old Westminsters: a biographical list of all those who are known to have been educated at Westminster School from Play 1883 to Election 1960.* Barnet: Stellar Press, 1963. Described as vol.3. Supersedes the supplementary volume issued in 1937.

PAGAN, F.E., & PAGAN, H.E. *The record of old Westminsters: a biographical list of all those who are known to have been educated at Westminster School from Play 1919 to Election 1989.* Westminster School Society, 1992. Described as vol.4.

PAGAN, F.E. *A supplementary volume to the Record of Old Westminsters, comprising Part I: Addenda and corrigenda to volume III. Part II: A biographical list of all those admitted to the School from Lent term 1961 to Play term 1974.* Hatfield: Stellar Press, 1978.

B. Further and Higher Education, etc.

Bedford College

TUKE, MARGARET J. *A history of Bedford College for Women 1849-1937.* Oxford University Press, 1939. Includes various lists of names, and biographical notes.

A catalogue of the archives of Bedford College (University of London), 1849-1985. The College, 1987. Includes lists of records relating to staff and students.

Birkbeck College

WARMINGTON, E.H. *A history of Birkbeck College, during the Second World-War, 1939-45.* Birkbeck College, 1954. Includes roll of honour.

City and Guilds College

CLUBB, CLARE M. 'The archives of the City and Guilds of London Institute', *Journal of the Society of Archivists* **8**, 1986, 124-6. These include records of staff and students, and information on examination candidates 1917-34.

WALKER, JOHN. *Register of students of the City and Guilds College, 1884-1934.* The College, 1936. In chronological order; includes much biographical information.

Gresham College

WARD, JOHN. *Lives of the professors of Gresham College.* John Moore, 1740. Extensive biographies; includes pedigree of Gresham of Norfolk, London and Surrey, 14-16th c.

Homerton College

HARDINGES, JOAN. 'Homerton College', *C.A.* **35**, 1987, 7-10. Training college for Congregational teachers; includes census schedule for 1871.

London University

LONDON UNIVERSITY. *The historical record (1836-1936).* University of London Press, 1926. Includes lists of graduates, prize winners, *etc.*

Manchester New College

Lists of professors, lecturers and principal officers, and roll of students of the Manchester New College, London, 1866-1889; Manchester New College, Oxford, 1889-1893; Manchester College, Oxford, 1893-1899. Manchester: H. Rawson, 1900. Roll of students entered at the Manchester Academy, 1786-1803; Manchester College, York, 1803-1840; Manchester New College, Manchester, 1840-1853; Manchester New College, London, 1853-1867; with a list of the professors and principal officers. Manchester: Johnson and Rawson, 1868.

Royal College of Science

OLD STUDENTS ASSOCIATION. Royal College of Science, London: register of old students. 2nd ed. Lamley & Co., 1912.

Royal School of Mines

Register of the Associates and old students of the Royal School of Mines. Royal School of Mines (Old Students) Association, 1947. There are also annual supplements.

University College

CHAMBERS, R.W., ed. This book is a record of those members of University College, London & of University College Hospital and Medical School who were killed or who died on service, 1914-1919. 2 vols. War Memorial Committee, 1922-4. Biographies.

Westfield College

SONDHEIMER, J. Castle Adamant in Hampstead: a history of Westfield College, 1882-1982. Westfield College, 1983. A womens' college of the University of London; includes biographical notes on a few prominent members.

Scriveners

STEER, FRANCIS W. A history of the Worshipful Company of Scriveners of London. Phillimore, 1973. General account with some extracts from accounts.

STEER, FRANCES W., ed. Scriveners' Company common paper, 1357-1628, with a continuation to 1678. L.R.S. 4. 1968. Includes many lists of masters, servants, apprentices, etc.

Sculptors

See Painters

Seamen

HARRIS, G.G. The Trinity House of Deptford, 1514-1660. Athlone Press, 1969. General history, with lists of masters and brethren, and list of sources.

SHILTON, DOROTHY O., & HOLWORTHY, RICHARD., eds. High Court of Admiralty examinations (ms volume 53) 1637-1638. 2 vols. New York: Anglo-American Research Foundation, 1932. Many relate to seamen of London.

See also Soldiers

Servants

KENT, D.A. 'Ubiquitous but invisible: female domestic servants in mid-eighteenth century London', History workshop 28, 1989, 111-28. General discussion based on the settlement examinations of St.Martins in the Fields.

Shearmen

See Cloth Workers

Sheriffs

See Mayors, Sheriffs, Aldermen and Councillors

Shipbrokers / Owners

JEFFERY, ALBERT ERIC. The history of Scruttons: shipbrokers and shipowners 1802-1926; stevedores, master porters and cargo superintendants 1890-1967. Privately published, 1971. Includes list of 'senior dock staff'.

WOOLF, MAURICE. 'Eighteenth century London shipowners', Transactions of the Jewish Historical Society of England 24, 1974, 198-204. Includes list.

Shipbuilders

BANBURY, PHILIP. Shipbuilders of the Thames and Medway. Newton Abbot: David & Charles, 1971. General history, noting a few names.

Shopkeepers

See Tradesmen

Shipwrights

RIDGE, C. HAROLD. *Records of the Worshipful Company of Shipwrights, being an alphabetical digest of freemen and apprentices, &c., compiled from the Company's records.* 2 vols. Phillimore & Co., 1939-46. v.1. 1428 to 1780. v.2. 1728 to 1858.

Silk Weavers

ROTHSTEIN, NATALIE. 'The Warner archive', *Pr.Hug.Soc.L.* **22**(3), 283-6. Notes on an archival collection relating to silk weavers.

Silversmiths

GLANVILLE, PHILIPPA, & GOLDSBOROUGH, JENNIFER FAULDS. *Women silversmiths, 1685-1845: works from the collection of the National Museum of Women in the Arts, Washington, D.C.* Thames and Hudson, 1990. Includes 'biographical list' of 300 women — two-thirds of them Londoners.

HOWARD, MONTAGUE. *Old London silver: its history, its makers and its marks.* New York: Charles Scibner's Sons, 1903. Includes list of silversmiths and makers marks.

See also Goldsmiths

Skinners

COKAYNE, GEORGE, EDWARD, ed. 'Skinners Company: apprenticeships', *M.G.H.* 3rd series **1**, 1896, 41-6, 76-80, 102-5, 149-52, 172-6, 194-6 & 246-53. Extracts, 1496-1515 and 1547-1694.

HERBERT, WILLIAM; *History of the Worshipful Company of Skinners, principally compiled from their own records.* J. & C. Adlard, 1837. Includes much information on charitable trusts, *etc.*

LAMBERT, JOHN JAMES, ed. *Records of the Skinners of London, Edward I to James I.* Worshipful Company of Skinners, 1933. Includes accounts with many names.

WADMORE, JAMES FOSTER. *Some account of the Worshipful Company of Skinners of London, being the Guild or Fraternity of Corpus Christi.* Blades, East & Blades, 1902. Includes many extracts from original sources, with lists of officers, and biographical notes on members who became mayors.

WADMORE, J.F. 'Some account of the history and antiquities of the Worshipful Company of Skinners', *T.L.M.A.S.* **5**, 1881, 92-182. General history.

'Skinners Company freedoms', *M.G.H.* 3rd series **3**, 1900, 33-7 & 73-6. 1500-1694; includes list of members of the Company, 1537.

Smugglers

MANCHÉE, W.H. 'Some Huguenot smugglers: the impeachment of London silk merchants, 1698', *Pr.Hug.Soc.L.* **15**, 1934-7, 406-27. Includes a list of weavers, 1695/6.

Soldiers, Militiamen, etc.

There are many works dealing with London's soldiers — mainly regimental histories. The list which follows is not comprehensive, rather, it includes only those works which provide lists of names, such as rolls of honour, or other information of direct interest to the genealogist.

BARNES, R. MONEY. *The soldiers of London.* Imperial Services Library **6**. Seeley Service & Co., 1963. Includes lists of the various volunteer regiments, *etc.* General background.

DILLON, HAROLD ARTHUR. 'On a ms. list of officers of the London trained bands in 1643', *Archaeologia* **52**, 1890, 129-44. Includes transcript.

EMBERTON, WILFRID. *Skippon's brave boys: the origins, development and Civil War service of London's trained bands.* Buckingham: Barracuda, 1984. Includes names of some soldiers.

LESLIE, J.H. 'Monuments and memorials of soldiers in the London city churches', *Journal of the Society for Army Historical Research* **4**, 1925, 145-9; **6**, 1927, 178-81. Brief.

LESLIE, J.H. 'A survey, or muster, of the armed and trayned companies in London, 1588 and 1599', *Journal of the Society for Army Historical Research* **4**, 1925, 62-71. Gives names of captains of each ward.

ROBERTS, KEITH. *London & liberty: ensigns of the London trained bands.* Partizan Press, 1987. Includes various lists of 17th c. officers.

ROBINSON, RICHARD. 'A survey, or muster, of the armed and trayned companies in London, 1588 and 1599', ed. J.H. Leslie. *Journal of the Society for Army Historical Research* **4**, 1925, 62-71. Lists captains and ensigns for each ward.

WALKER, G. GOOLD. 'Huguenots in the trained bands of London and the Honourable Artillery Company', *Pr.Hug.Soc.L.* **15**, 1934-7, 300-316. Includes list, mainly 17-18th c.

'Old memorials of British seamen and soldiers in London', *Journal of the Royal United Service Institute* **66**, 1921, 481-5. Brief list of some older memorials.

47th (London) Division

MAUDE, ALAN H., ed. *The 47th (London) Division 1914-1919* Amalgamated Press (1922) Ltd., 1922. Includes honours list.

Artists Rifles

HIGHAM, S. STAGOL. *The regimented roll of honour and war record of the Artists Rifles (1/28th, 2/28th and 3/28th Battalions, the London Regiment T.F.) Commissions, promotions, appointments and rewards for service in the field obtained by members of the Corps since 4th August 1914.* 3rd ed. Howlett & Son, 1922. Includes extensive lists of names.

City Imperial Volunteers

SCOTT, BUY H. GUILLUM, & McDONELL, GEOFFREY, eds. *The record of the Mounted Infantry of the City Imperial Volunteers.* E. & F.M. Spon, 1902. Boer War; includes nominal roll.

Ealing and Brentford Volunteers

RIVIS, R.G.L. 'The Ealing and Brentford Volunteers', *Local historian [Ealing Local History Society]* **5**, 1965, 11-14. Lists officers, 1803-4.

Honourable Artillery Company

RAIKES, G.A. *The ancient vellum book of the Honourable Artillery Company, being the roll of members, from 1611 to 1682.* Richard Bentley & Son, 1890.

RAIKES, G.A. *The history of the Honourable Artillery Company.* 2 vols. Richard Bentley & Son, 1878-9. Includes various lists of officers, *etc.*

WALKER, G. GOOLD. *The Honourable Artillery Company, 1537-1947.* Aldershot: Gale and Polden, 1954. Includes various rolls of honour, 20th c.

WALKER, G. GOOLD. *The Honourable Artillery Company in the Great War, 1914-1919.* Seeley Service & Co., 1930. Includes extensive roll of honour, *etc.*

WILLIAMS, BASIL, & CHILDERS, ERSKINE. *The H.A.C. in South Africa: a record of the services rendered by members of the Honourable Artillery Company.* Smith Elder, 1903. Includes 'Alphabetical list of members of the H.A.C. who served in South Africa'.

See also London Regiment

Imperial Yeomanry

MOORE, WILLIAM E.D. 'The South African War: the 34th Company (Middlesex) Imperial Yeomanry', *Metropolitan* **17**(4), 1995, 57-9. Includes roll of officers and men, 1900-1901.

REW, H.G. MACKENZIE. *Records of the Rough Riders (XXth Battalion), Imperial Yeomanry, Boer War, 1899-1902.* Bedford: Brown & Wilson, 1907. Includes nominal roll.

Inns of Court

DARLING, CHARLES. *Inner Templars who volunteered and served in the Great War.* Chiswick Press, [1924]. Roll of enlistment; includes soldiers and sailors.

ERRINGTON, FRANCIS H.L. *The Inns of Court Officer Training Corps during the Great War.* Printing-Craft, 1922. Includes extensive records of rank and file, including addresses.

The war book of Gray's Inn, containing names of members who served, with biographical notices of those who fell ... Butterworth, 1921.

See also London Regiment

Light Horse Volunteers

COLLYER, JAMES NICOLSON, & POCOCK, JOHN INNES. *An historical record of the Light Horse Volunteers of London and Westminster, with the muster rolls from the first formation of the Regiment, MDCCLXIX, to the relodgement of the standards in the Tower, MDCCCXXIX.* Wright, 1843.

London Irish

The London Irish at war: a history of the battalions of the London Irish Rifles in World War II. London Irish Rifles Old Comrades Association, [1949]. Includes roll of honour and list of awards.

London Regiment

BAILEY, O.F., & HOLLIER, H.M. *The Kensingtons, 13th London Regiment.* Regimental Old Comrades Association, [1936]. First World War history; includes roll of honour.

EAMES, F.W. *The Second Nineteenth, being the history of the 2/19th London Regiment.* Waterlow & Sons, 1931. Includes casualty lists, 1916-18, *etc.*

ELLIOT, W.R. *The second twentieth, being the history of the 2/20th Bn. London Regiment.* Aldershot: Gale & Polden, 1920. Includes roll of honour, 1616 and 1918, nominal roll of officers, 1916, *etc.*

PLANCK, C. DUDLEY. *History of the 7th (City of London) Battalion, the London Regiment, embracing the 3rd London and the 32nd Searchlight Regiment, R.A., (7th City of London).* Old Comrades Association, 1946. Includes roll of honour, 1914-18.

The 23rd London Regiment, 1789-1919. Times Publishing, 1936. Includes list of casualties, 1914-19.

Soldiers died in the Great War, 1914-1918, pt.76: the London Regiment, Honourable Artillery Company (Infantry), Inns of Court Officers Training Corps. H.M.S.O., 1921. Reprinted Polstead: J.B. Hayward & Co., 1988.

London Rifle Brigade

DURAND, A.T.M., & HASTINGS, R.H.W.S. *The London Rifle Brigade, 1919-50.* Aldershot: Gale and Polden, 1952. Includes roll of honour and list of decorations, *etc.*

MAURICE, SIR FREDERICK. *The history of the London Rifle Brigade, 1859-1919.* Constable & Co., 1921. Includes nominal roll of officers with brief biographical notes, plus various other lists.

London Scottish

BARCLAY, C.N., ed. *The London Scottish in the Second World War, 1939 to 1945.* William Clowes & Sons, 1952.

LINDSAY, J.H. *The London Scottish in the Great War.* Regimental Headquarters, 1925. Includes roll of honour.

Middlesex Regiment

KEMP, PETER. *The Middlesex Regiment (Duke of Cambridge's Own), 1919-1952.* Aldershot: Gale & Polden, 1956. Includes roll of honour and list of honours and awards, 1939-1952.

KING, E.J. *The history of the 7th Battalion Middlesex Regiment.* Harrison & Sons, 1927. Includes various lists of officers, 1859-1927.

KINGSFORD, CHARLES LETHBRIDGE. *The story of the Duke of Cambridge's Own (Middlesex Regiment).* George Newnes, 1916. Covers 1755-1916; includes roll of honour, 1914-16, and list of serving officers, August 1916.

Roll of honour of the officers, warrant officers, non-commissioned officers, and men of the Middlesex Regiment (Duke of Cambridge's Own) who were killed in the Great War, 1914-18. Aldershot: Gale & Polden, [192-?].

Soldiers died in the Great War, part 56: the Duke of Cambridge's Own (Middlesex Regiment). H.M.S.O., 1921.

Middlesex Rifle Volunteers

EVANS, E.T. *Records of the third Middlesex Rifle Volunteers, and of the various corps which formed the second & sixth Middlesex administrative battalions ... 1794 to 1884.* Simpkin Marshall & Co., 1885. Includes various lists of officers.

RUDD, COLOUR SERGEANT. *The early history of the 17th (North) Middlesex Volunteer Rifles, (formerly the 29th), 1859 to 1889.* R. & J. Widdicombe, 1895. Includes a number of portraits.

Middlesex Yeomanry

STONHAM, CHARLES, & FREEMAN, BENSON. *Historical records of the Middlesex Yeomanry, 1797-1927.* ed. J.S. Judd. Regimental Committee, 1930. Includes list of 55 men lost in the Boer War, 1900-1902.

National Guard

FOSTER, A.E. MANNING. *The National Guard in the Great War, 1914-1918.* Cope & Fenwick, 1920. London company; many names.

54

Prince of Wales Own Civil Service Rifles

The history of the Prince of Wales' Own Civil Service Rifles. The Regiment, 1921. 15th Battalion London Regiment. Includes list of 'officers who served in the period 1914-1919', and various other lists.

Queen Victoria's Rifles

KEESON, CUTHBERT A.G.C. *The history and records of Queen Victoria's Rifles, 1792-1922.* Constable & Co., 1923. From 1908, the London Regiment, 9th (County of London) Battalion. Includes roll of honour, 1915-17.

Queen's Westminster Rifles

HENRIQUES, J.Q. *The war history of the 1st Battalion Queens Westminster Rifles, 1914-1918.* Medici Society, 1923. 16th (County of London) Battalion, the London Regiment. Includes roll of honour.

Rangers

WHEELER-HOLOHAN, A.V., & WYATT, G.M.G. *The Rangers historical records: from 1859 to the conclusion of the Great War.* Harrison & Sons, [1921]. Includes list of honours and awards, 1st World War.

Royal Artillery

FARMER, HENRY GEORGE. *History of the Royal Artillery Band, 1762-1953.* Royal Artillery Institution, 1954. Includes various lists of officers, instrumentalists, *etc.*

GRIMWOOD, B.J. *The history of the 53rd (London) Medium Brigade, Royal Artillery.* South Darenth: Little Boys Press, [1936]. 19-20th c., includes a few names.

JOCELYN, JULIAN R.J. *The history of the Royal and Indian Artillery in the mutiny of 1857.* John Murray, 1915. Includes various lists of officers.

JOCELYN, JULIAN R.J. *The history of the Royal Artillery, Crimean period.* John Murray, 1911. Includes various lists of names.

LESLIE, J.H. *Calendar of inscriptions upon monuments, tombstones, etc., relating to officers of the Royal Artillery.* Supplement to *Proceedings of the Royal Artillery Institution* **27-9**, 1900-1903.

List of officers of the Royal Regiment of Artillery from the year 1716 to the year 1899, to which are added the notes on officers services collected by General W.H. Askwith. 4th ed. Royal Artillery Institution, 1900. For the period from 1862, this is superseded by:

List of officers of the Royal Regiment of Artillery from June 1862 to June 1914. New ed. Sheffield: Sir W.C. Leng & Co., 1914. Described as vol.2, but vol.1 was not published.

Royal Fusiliers

GREY, W.E. *The 2nd City of London Regiment (Royal Fusiliers) in the Great War, (1914-19).* The Regiment, 1929. Includes roll of honour.

S[HIPLEY], C.A.L. *The Royal Fusiliers, (City of London Regiment): history of the 2nd Battallion in North Africa, Italy and Greece, March, 1943-May, 1945.* Aldershot: Gale & Polden, 1946. Includes various lists of officers.

Soldiers died in the Great War, part 12: the Royal Fusiliers (City of London Regiment). H.M.S.O., 1921.

University of London O.T.C.

University of London Officers Training Corps: roll of war service, 1914-1919. University of London Military Education Committee, 1921. Extensive.

West Middlesex Regiment of Foot

WARRE, H.J. *Historical records of the Fifty-Seventh, or, West Middlesex Regiment of Foot; compiled from official and private sources, from the date of its formation in 1755, to the present time, 1878.* W. Mitchell & Co., 1878. Includes various lists of officers and men.

WOOLLRIGHT, H.H. *History of the Fifty-Seventh (West Middlesex) Regiment of Foot.* Gale & Polden, 1907.

Yeomen of the Guard

PAGET, JULIAN. *The Yeomen of the Guard: five hundred years of service 1485-1985.* Poole: Blandford Press, 1984. Includes lists of the Body Guard in 1485 and 1984, and list of captains, 1485-1984.

Solicitors
See Lawyers

Spectacle Makers
COURT, THOMAS H. & ROHR, MORITZ VON. 'Contributions to the history of the Worshipful Company of Spectaclemakers', *Optical Society transactions* **31**, 1929-30, 53-90. Includes 'chronological list of the more important members ... including the leading independent opticians'.

LAW, FRANK W. *The Worshipful Company of Spectacle Makers: a history.* The Company, 1979. Includes list of masters, 1629-1977, and clerks, 1629-1966.

WEBB, CLIFF. *London livery company apprenticeship registers, volume 14. Spectaclemakers Company 1666-1800; Loriners' Company 1722-1731; 1759-1800.* Society of Genealogists, 1998.

Spicers
See Pepperers

Spoonmakers
KENT, TIMOTHY ARTHUR. *London silver spoonmakers, 1500 to 1697.* Silver Society, 1981. Biographical notes.

Staple Officials
RICH, E.E. 'List of officials of the Staple of Westminster', *Cambridge historical journal* **4**, 1932-4, 192-3. List, 1353-1532.

Stevedores
LOVELL, JOHN. *Stevedores and dockers: a study of trade unionism in the Port of London, 1870-1914.* Macmillan, 1969. Includes useful bibliography.
See also Shipbrokers / owners

Stockbrokers
A list of the brokers of the City of London ... Henry Fenwick, 1814-42. Irregular; 8 issues.

Students
See School Pupils and Teachers

Surgeons
See Medical Professions

Surgical Instrument Makers
See Medical Professions

Surveyors
See Local Government Officers

Swan Owners
TICEHURST, NORMAN F. 'The marks used by swan-owners of London and Middlesex', *The London naturalist: the journal of the London Natural History Society* 1933, 67-84. List, with names.

Sword Blade Makers
TOFTS-WHITE, JOHN. 'The sword-blade makers at Hounslow sword mill', *Honeslaw chronicle* **3**(2), 1980, 18-22; **6**(1), 1983, 12-15.

Tailors
GIEVE, DAVID W. *Gieves and Hawkes, 1785-1985: the story of a tradition.* Gieves & Hawkes, 1985. History of a firm of tailors; includes pedigree of Gieves, 18-20th c., also list of long-serving staff.

LEVITT, SARAH. *Victorians unbuttoned: registered designs for clothing, their makers and wearers, 1839-1900.* Allen & Unwin, 1986. Includes list of patentees.

MARLY, DIANA DE. 'Fashionable suppliers 1660-1700: leading tailors and clothing tradesmen of the Restoration period', *Antiquaries journal* **58**, 1979, 333-51.

Tallow Chandlers
MONIER-WILLIAMS, M.F., ed. *Records of the Worshipful Company of Tallow Chandlers, London.* Chiswick Press, 1897. General history, with many extracts from deeds, *etc.*

MONIER-WILLIAMS, RANDALL. *The Tallow Chandlers of London.* 4 vols. Kaye & Ward, 1970-77. General history.

Tanners
See Drovers

Tapestry Weavers
HEFFORD, WENDY. 'Soho and Spitalfields: little-known Huguenot tapestry weavers in and around London, 1680-1780', *Proceedings of the Huguenot Society of London* **24**(2), 1984, 103-12.

Tax Officials

Returns of the names of the several persons employed in the assessment and collection of income tax, and land and assessed taxes, in the City of London, during the year ended on the 5th day of April 1855 ... House of Commons Parliamentary papers 1854-5, XXX, 477-9. Similar returns were made for 1855 (1856, XXXVIII, 483-5), 1856 (1857, XXV, 295-7) and 1857 (1857-8, XXXIV, 107-9).

Teachers

See School Pupils and Teachers

Theatrical Personnel

HONIGMANN, E.A.J., & BROCK, SUSAN, eds. *Playhouse wills, 1558-1642: an edition of wills by Shakespeare and his contemporaries in the London theatre.* Manchester: Manchester University Press, 1993. Wills of numerous actors, theatre owners, dramatists, and other theatrical personnel.

HOWARD, DIANA. *London's theatres and music halls, 1850-1950.* Library Association, 1970. Gazetteer, giving names of managers; also includes bibliography.

KNIGHT, WILLIAM G. *A major London 'Minor': the Surrey Theatre, 1805-1865.* Society for Theatre Research, 1997. Includes much information on personnel, with 'Surrey Theatre pay-list for week ending Friday, 18th October, 1861'.

See also Actors

Thief Takers

PALEY, RUTH. 'Thief-takers in London in the age of the McDaniel gang, c.1745-1754', in HAY, DOUGLAS, & SNYDER, FRANCIS, eds. *Policing and prosecution in Britain, 1750-1850.* Oxford: Clarendon Press, 1989, 301-41. Includes list of 'thief-takers'.

Tinplate Workers

EBBLEWHITE, ERNEST ARTHUR. *A chronological history of the Worshipful Company of Tin-plate Workers, alias wire-workers, of the City of London, from the date of its incorporation to the present time.* The Company, 1896. Lists masters, wardens, *etc.,* from 1670; also list of livery, 1895.

WARNER, OLIVER. *A history of the Tin Plate Workers alias Wire Workers Company of the City of London.* S. Straker & Sons, 1964. Includes list of masters and clerks, 1670-1964, *etc.*

WEBB, CLIFF. *London livery company apprenticeship registers, volume 16. Tinplateworkers' Company 1666, 1668, 1676, 1681, 1683-1800.* Society of Genealogists, 1998.

Tradesmen

An exceptionally wide variety of trades have been practised in London. Many historic trades — from scrivener to cork-cutter, from sail-maker to wheeler — are described in:

CAMPBELL, R. *The London tradesman.* Newton Abbot: David & Charles, 1969. Facsimile reprint. Originally published 1747.

For what is essentially an eighteenth-century directory of tradesmen, see:

MORTIMOR, Mr. *The universal director, or, the nobleman and gentleman's true guide to the masters and proffessors of the liberal and public arts and sciences, and of the mechanic arts, manufactures and trades established in London and Westminster and their environs.* 3 vols. J. Coote, 1763. Essentially a directory of tradesmen.

Early 19th c. tradesmen are listed in: 'Leading tradesmen of London in 1830', *Genealogical quarterly* **5,** 1936-7, 279-88 & 327-64; **6,** 1938-9, 464-85, 538-62, 599-620 & 669-90; **7,** 1938-9, 33-58, 71-105, 159-93 & 288-302; **8,** 1939-40, 53-62 & 182-9.

Tradesmen's tokens, cards and signboards all provide much potentially useful information. They have been subjected to detailed examination, resulting in the publication of a number of valuable works which include many names:

Signboards

HEAL, AMBROSE, SIR. *The signboards of old London shops: a review of the shop signs employed by the London tradesmen during the XVIIth and XVIIIth centuries ...* B.T. Batsford, 1947. Reprinted Portman Books, 1988. Includes extensive 'index of shopkeepers' names'.

HEAL, AMBROSE, SIR. *London shop-signs, other than those given by Larwood & Hotten in their 'History of Signboards'.* [ ], 1939. Reprinted from *Notes & queries* **176**, 1939, *passim.* Many names of tradesmen given.

NORMAN, PHILIP. *London signs and inscriptions.* Elliot Stock, 1893. Supplemented by his 'Additional notes on London sculptured and carved signs, coats-of-arms and inscriptions', *Journal of the British Archaeological Association* N.S., **21**, 1915, 97-142.

PRICE, F.G. HILTON. 'Signs of old London', *L.T.R.* **2**, 1903, 70-108; **3**, 1906, 110-65; **4**, 1907, 27-111; **5**, 1908, 145-87. Lists tradesmen's signboards, with their names, mainly 17-18th c.

Duck Lane

CUMING, H. SYER. 'Old traders' signs in Duck Lane', *Journal of the British Archaeological Association* **49**, 1893, 117-9. Includes names, 17-18th c.

Little Britain

CUMING, H. SYER. 'Old traders' signs in Little Britain', *Journal of the British Archaeological Association* **49**, 1893, 108-16. 17-18th c.

Lombard Street

PRICE, F.G. HILTON. *The signs of old Lombard Street.* Rev.ed. Leadenhall Press, 1902. Gives names of occupants, mainly 18-19th c.

London Bridge

CUMING, H. SYER. 'Traders signs on Old London Bridge', *Journal of the British Archaeological Association* **43**, 1887, 162-73. 16-18th c.

Paternoster Row

CUMING, H. SYER. 'The old traders' signs in Paternoster Row', *Journal of the British Archaeological Association* **41**, 1885, 278-83. 16-18th c.

St.Michael, Crooked Lane

HILL, R.H. ERNEST. 'London signs, 1638', *H.C.M.* **8**, 1906, 62-4. Lists traders in the parish of St.Michael, Crooked Lane.

St.Pauls Churchyard

CUMING, H. SYER. 'On the old traders' signs in St.Pauls Churchyard', *Journal of the British Archaeological Association* **39**, 1883, 241-54. Many names, 16-18th c.

Strand

PRICE, F.G. HILTON. 'The signs of the old houses in the Strand in the 17th & 18th centuries', *M.H.N.Q.* **2**, 1896, 10-13, 93-6, 119-22 & 155-60; **3**, 1897, 17-19, 78-9, 116-20 & 196-9; **4**, 1898, 126-8. Names a variety of tradesmen.

Westminster Hall

CUMING, H. SYER. 'The old traders' signs in Westminster Hall', *Journal of the British Archaeological Association* **42**, 1886, 137-42.

Tradesmen's Cards

HEAL, AMBROSE. *London tradesmen's cards of the XVIII century: an account of their origin and use.* New York: Dover, 1968.

HEAL, AMBROSE. *Old London Bridge tradesmen's cards and tokens.* John Love, 1931. Reprinted from HOME, GORDON. *Old London Bridge.*

Tradesmen's Tokens

AKERMAN, JOHN YONGE. *Tradesmen's tokens current in London and its vicinity between the years 1648 and 1672 ...* John Russell Smith, 1849.

BURN, JACOB HENRY. *A descriptive catalogue of the London traders, tavern and coffeehouse tokens current in the seventeenth century, presented to the Corporation Library by Henry Benjamin Hanbury Beaufoy ...* 2nd ed. Corporation of the City of London, 1855.

FRANKS, A.W. *London tokens of the 17th century.* Numismatic Society of London, 1862.

ROGERS, KENNETH. 'Issuers of 17th cent London tokens whose names were not known to Boyne and Williamson', *Numismatic chronicle* 5th series **8**, 1928, 61-97 & 338.

SQUIBB, T.F.E. 'Seventeenth century trade tokens for the County of Middlesex', *M.L.H.C.B.* **16**, 1963, 6-12. Includes brief list.

WATERS, ARTHUR W. *Notes gleaned from contemporary literature, &c., respecting the issuers of the eighteenth century tokens, struck for the County of Middlesex, arranged according to Atkins's Trademens tokens.* Leamington Spa: Simmons & Waters, 1906.

Transport Workers

TEDMAN, C.H. 'London Transport archives', *Sussex family historian* 12(2), 1996, 73-5. List staff records.

Trumpet Makers

BYRNE, MAURICE. 'The goldsmith-trumpet makers of the British Isles', *Galpin Society journal* 19, 1966, 71-83. Mainly of London. Includes biographical notes.

Turners

CHAMPNESS, ROLAND. *The Worshipful Company of Turners of London.* Lindley-Jones and Brother, 1966. Includes list of masters and wardens, *etc.*

STANLEY-STONE, A.C. *The Worshipful Company of Turners of London: its origin and history.* Lindley-Jones & Brother, 1925. Includes lists of masters, wardens, clerks, *etc.,* with 'list of livery', giving addresses of members in 1925.

Tylers

BELL, WALTER GEORGE. *A short history of the Worshipful Company of Tylers and Bricklayers of the City of London.* H.G. Montgomery, 1938. Includes list of masters, 16-20th c.

WEBB, CLIFF. *London livery companies apprenticeship registers, volume 2. Tylers' and Bricklayers' Company, 1612-1644, 1668-1800.* Society of Genealogists, 1996.

Undertakers

Undertakers, Middlesex. 1 microfiche. London & North Middlesex F.H.S., 1990. List of undertakers from the burial registers of Wesley's Chapel, City Road, 1779-1854.

Underwriters

SAMUEL, WILFRED S. 'Tentative list of Jewish underwriting members of Lloyds (from some time prior to 1800 until the year 1901)', *Miscellanies of the Jewish Historical Society of England* 5, 1948, 176-92.

Upholsterers

WEBB, CLIFF. *London livery company apprenticeships registers Volume 19. Upholders' Company, 1704-1772.* Society of Genealogists, 1998

WALTON, KARIN M. 'The Worshipful Company of Upholders of the City of London', *Furniture history: the journal of the Furniture History Society* 9, 1973, 41-79. Includes list of freedom admissions, 1698-1803.

Victims

NEAL, WENDY. *With disastrous consequences: London disasters, 1830-1917.* Enfield Lock: Hisarlik Press, 1992. Includes appendix listing all identified victims.

KENDALL, DOREEN. 'The Bethnal Green tube disaster', *East London record* 15, 1992, 27-33. Lists 173 victims of a war-time accident.

Vintners

CRAWFORD, ANNE. *A history of the Vintners' Company.* Constable, 1977. Includes lists of officers, *etc.*

MILBOURN, THOMAS. *The Vintners' Company: their muniments, plate and eminent members, with some account of the Ward of Vintry.* The Company, 1888. Includes biographical notes on eminent members, list of masters, *etc.*

MILBOURN, THOMAS. 'Biographical notices of some eminent members of the Vintners Company', *T.L.M.A.S.* 3, 1870, 448-71.

Violin Makers

FIRTH, JILLIAN. *A violin maker's map of London 1650-1850.* London College of Furniture, 1979. Biographical dictionary, with folded sheet map in folder.

Watchmakers

BUCKLEY, FRANCIS. *Old watchmakers III: of London, 1600-1750.* Uppermill, Yorkshire: Moore & Edwards, 1929. Brief.

59

Watermen

COTTRELL, ROBERT J. *Surname index to the Company of Watermen and Lightermen, London.* 9 folders + fiche. Bexleyheath: R.J.Cottrell, [1991]-6. Apprenticeship bindings, 1692-1949.
This index is discussed in:
COTTRELL, ROB. 'Indexers and their indexes: Thames watermen and lightermen', *Family tree magazine* **9**(12), 1993, 27-8.
HUMPHERUS, HENRY. *History of the origin and progress of the Company of Watermen and Lightermen of the River Thames.* 3 vols. S. Prentice, [1887-9]. Extensive general history.

Wax Chandlers

WEBB, CLIFF. *London Livery company apprenticeship registers volume 31. Wax Chandlers Company, 1666-1800, & Brown Bakers Company, 1615-46.* Society of Genealogists, 2000. Not seen.
DUMMELOW, JOHN. *The Wax Chandlers of London: a short history of the Worshipful Company of Wax Chandlers, London.* Phillimore, 1973. Includes list of records, extracts from accounts, list of masters, *etc.*

Weavers

CONSITT, FRANCES. *The London Weavers Company.* Oxford: Clarendon Press, 1933. Vol.1. From the twelfth century to the close of the sixteenth century. No more published. Includes many extracts from accounts, *etc.*
PLUMMER, ALFRED. *The London Weavers Company, 1600-1970.* Routledge & Kegan Paul, 1972. Includes list of Company records, list of upper bailiffs, *etc.*
RADCLIFFE, F.R.Y. 'List of Wiltshiremen extracted from the minute books of the Company of Weavers of London, 1653-1674', *Wiltshire archaeological magazine* **38**(122), 1914, 572-5.
WALLER, WILLIAM CHAPMAN, ed. *Extracts from the court book of the Weavers Company of London, 1610-1730.* P.Hg.S.L. **33**, 1931.
See also Tapestry Weavers

Wheelwrights

BENNETT, ERIC. *The Worshipful Company of Wheelwrights of the City of London, 1670-1970.* Newton Abbot: David & Charles, 1970. Includes lists of masters and clerks since 1670.
SCOTT, JAMES B. *A short account of the Worshipful Company of Wheelwrights.* The Company, 1884. Includes list of livery, 1884, and of masters, 1670-1884.
SCOTT, JAMES B. *A list of masters, wardens, court of assistants, and livery, of the Worshipful Company of Wheelwrights of the City of London, with a short account of the Wheelwrights Company.* [The Company?, 1889. List of livery in 1889.

Wind Instrument Makers

LANGWILL, LYNDESAY G. 'London wind instrument makers of the seventeenth and eighteenth centuries', *Music review* **7**, 1947, 88-102. General discussion, with some names.

Wire Drawers

GLOVER, ELIZABETH. *The gold & silver wyre-drawers.* Chichester: Phillimore, 1979. Includes lists of masters, clerks and beadles since 1693.
STEWART, HORACE. *History of the Worshipful Company of Gold and Silver Wyre-Drawers, and of the development of the industry which the Company represents.* Leadenhall Press, 1891. Includes lists of masters, clerks and beadles, and of members in 1891.

Woolmen

DE BRUYNE, H.B.A. *A history of the Woolmen's Company.* Privately printed, 1964. Includes list of sources, and roll of masters, 1661-1964.
See also Glass Makers & Sellers

Zoo Keepers

WEINSTEIN, ROSEMARY. 'Some menagerie accounts of James I', *T.L.M.A.S.* **31**, 1980, 133-41. Accounts naming those responsible for the royal menagerie.

Author Index

68

Family Name Index

Place Name Index

71